Anonymous

A Testimonial to Charles J. Paine and Edward Burgess

Vol. 1

Anonymous

A Testimonial to Charles J. Paine and Edward Burgess
Vol. 1

ISBN/EAN: 9783337427870

Printed in Europe, USA, Canada, Australia, Japan

Cover: Foto ©ninafisch / pixelio.de

More available books at **www.hansebooks.com**

A TESTIMONIAL

TO

CHARLES J. PAINE

AND

EDWARD BURGESS,

FROM THE

CITY OF BOSTON,

FOR THEIR SUCCESSFUL DEFENCE OF THE
AMERICA'S CUP.

BOSTON:
PRINTED BY ORDER OF THE CITY COUNCIL.
1887.

CITY OF BOSTON.

In Board of Aldermen, Oct. 10, 1887.

Ordered, That the Clerk of Committees be authorized to prepare for publication, under the direction of the Committee on Printing, an appropriate memorial volume, giving an account of the action of the City Council, and the reception at Faneuil Hall by the City of Boston, to Charles J. Paine, owner, and Edward Burgess, designer, of the yacht *Volunteer*, including biographical sketches of said gentlemen; and that the same be printed, the expense incurred thereby to be charged to the appropriation for Printing.

Passed. Sent down for concurrence.

In Common Council, Oct. 13, 1887.

Concurred.
Approved by the Mayor October 15, 1887.
A true copy.

Attest: JOHN T. PRIEST.
Assistant City Clerk.

CONTENTS.

	PAGE
INTRODUCTORY HISTORY	9-84
Victory of the *America*	11
Description of the *America* (Note)	17
First International Race, 1870	20
Second International Race, 1871	22
Third International Race, 1876	23
Fourth International Race, 1881	25
Deed of Gift of the America's Cup to the New York Yacht Club	26
The Challenge of the *Genesta*	29
The Boston Sloop *Puritan*	33
The English Cutter *Genesta*	37
The Trial Races of 1885	40
Summary of the First Race	41
Second Trial Race, and Summary	42
Third Trial Race, and Summary	43
The America's Cup Races of 1885	44
The First Race	48
Summary of the First Race	50
The Second Race	51
Summary of the Second Race	53
The Challenge of the *Galatea*	53
The Boston Sloop *Mayflower*	54
The English Cutter *Galatea*	58
The Trial Races of 1886	60
Summary of the First Race	61
Second Trial Race, and Summary	62
The America's Cup Races of 1886	63
The First Race	63

CONTENTS.

	PAGE
Summary of the First Race	66
The Second Race .	67
Summary of the Second Race	69
The Challenge of the *Thistle*	70
The Steel Sloop *Volunteer* .	70
The "Boston Herald" Cup (Note) .	73
The Scotch Cutter *Thistle* .	74
The Trial Race of 1887	77
Summary of the Race .	78
The America's Cup Races of 1887	78
The First Race .	78
Summary of the First Race .	81
The Second Race .	81
Summary of the Second Race .	83
Table of Contests for the America's Cup in American Waters,	84
THE AMERICA'S CUP .	87
New Deed of Gift of the Cup to the New York Yacht Club .	88
BIOGRAPHICAL SKETCH OF CHARLES J. PAINE .	95
BIOGRAPHICAL SKETCH OF EDWARD BURGESS	100
THE RECEPTION IN FANEUIL HALL	105–150
Committee on Reception .	105
Message from His Honor the Mayor to the City Council	108
Action of the City Council .	108
Address of His Honor the Mayor	116
Remarks of Charles J. Paine .	117
Remarks of Edward Burgess .	119
Remarks of His Excellency Governor Ames .	121
Remarks of Frederic O. Prince	121
Telegram from Marblehead	127
Remarks of William Everett .	128
Remarks of Henry B. Lovering	131
Remarks of Rev. E. A. Horton .	133
Remarks of Charles Levi Woodbury	135
Remarks of Rev. J. P. Bodfish .	136
Remarks and Poem by Rev. M. J. Savage	137
Remarks of Gen. N. P. Banks	140
Remarks of Thomas J. Gargan	144

CONTENTS.

	PAGE
Remarks of William E. Russell	147
Letter from Capt. H. C. Haff	148
Address of Welcome from "Dahlgren Post, No. 2, G.A.R."	149
CORRESPONDENCE, ETC.	151–159
Letter from Oliver Wendell Holmes	151
Letter from Benjamin F. Butler	151
Letter from Charles Devens	153
Letter from Henry Cabot Lodge	154
Letter from John M. Forbes	154
Letter from R. B. Forbes	155
Message from "Old Colony Club"	155
Message from "Sons of Martha's Vineyard"	155
Message from "New Bedford Yacht Club"	157
Letter from Rev. Phillips Brooks	157
Letter from Charles W. Eliot	157
Letter from Rev. James Freeman Clarke	158
Acknowledgment from Charles J. Paine	158
Reply of His Honor the Mayor to General Paine	159

LIST OF ILLUSTRATIONS.

	PAGE
THE AMERICA'S CUP	Frontispiece
THE SCHOONER *America* .	16
THE BOSTON SLOOP *Puritan* .	32
THE ENGLISH CUTTER *Genesta*	37
THE BOSTON SLOOP *Mayflower*	54
THE ENGLISH CUTTER *Galatea*	58
RACE BETWEEN THE *Mayflower* AND *Galatea*	63
THE BOSTON SLOOP *Volunteer*	70
THE SCOTCH CUTTER *Thistle* .	74
DIAGRAM OF SAILS .	83
PORTRAIT OF CHARLES J. PAINE	95
PORTRAIT OF EDWARD BURGESS	100
INTERIOR OF FANEUIL HALL .	112

INTRODUCTORY HISTORY

OF THE

INTERNATIONAL REGATTAS.

INTRODUCTORY HISTORY.

For the proper understanding of the meaning of the celebration recorded in these pages, a brief retrospect is necessary. The gentlemen who have been honored in this manner have been for three successive years the successful defenders of the "America's Cup;" hence the necessity of explaining what that trophy is.

The yacht *America* was undoubtedly the product of the excitement attendant upon the World's Fair at London, in 1851. National pride was excited by the competition opened in so many branches of industry, and, among other departments, that of ship-building was deeply stirred. American clippers and American pilot-boats had a great reputation for speed, and the most noted designer of the latter class of vessel was George Steers, of New York.

Com. John C. Stevens, of the New York Yacht Club, was the owner of the sloop-yacht *Maria*, built by Steers in 1846, which had proved the correctness of the theories of her designer. In 1851 Mr. Stevens and a few friends were easily induced to give an order to Mr. Steers for a new schooner, to be sent abroad to maintain the reputation of the American flag. No special challenge was issued by the British yacht clubs, but it was well understood that there would be many races sailed in British waters, and it was supposed that the stranger would have many chances to compete for prizes.

The result was that George Steers built the *America*, and took her across to Havre, where she was put into racing-trim. Thence she sailed to Cowes, Isle of Wight, a noted rendezvous for yachts, and prepared for business. Unfortunately the English cutter *Laverock* secured a trial-race, and, as Commodore Stevens wrote, "Not many hours after anchoring at Cowes it was well understood from the known capacity of the *Laverock* that certainly no schooner, and probably no cutter, of the Royal Yacht Squadron could beat the Yankee in sailing to windward in a moderate breeze."

The English yachtsmen were simply amazed and frightened by the new-comer, and were very slow in attempting to meet her. Commodore Stevens posted in the club-house at Cowes a challenge to sail the *America* in a match against any British vessel whatever, for any sum from one to ten thousand guineas, merely stipulating that there should be not less than a six-knot breeze.

This challenge was left open until the 17th of August, 1851; but no acceptance or reply to it was received.

On the 28th of August the *America* sailed against the schooner yacht *Titania*, owned by Robert Stephenson. The race was for £100, to sail twenty miles to windward and back, and the *America* won by nearly an hour. The *Titania*, however, was by no means a champion yacht, and this race decided nothing.

Failing in all other attempts to get a match, it was decided to enter the *America* in a regular regatta to be sailed for the Royal Yacht Squadron's Cup of £100. The newspapers of that date bear evidence to the intense interest excited by the contest, and we select the following account from the "London Illustrated News." From the same journal we have copied the very satisfactory picture which shows the *America* as she was at that time:—

"ROYAL YACHT SQUADRON REGATTA.— VICTORY OF THE
AMERICA.

"The race at Cowes, on Friday se'nnight, for the Royal Yacht Squadron Cup of £100, furnished our yachtsmen with an opportunity of 'realizing,' as our trans-atlantic brethren would say, what those same dwellers beyond the ocean can do afloat in competition with ourselves. None doubted that the *America* was a very fast sailer, but her powers had not been measured by the test of an actual contest. Therefore, when it became known that she was entered amongst the yachts to run for the cup on Friday, the most intense interest was manifested by all classes, from the highest to the humblest, who have thronged in such masses this season to the Isle of Wight; and even Her Majesty and the Court felt the influence of the universal curiosity which was excited to see how the stranger, of whom such great things were said, should acquit herself on the occasion. The race was, in fact, regarded as a sort of trial heat, from which some anticipation might be formed of the result of the great international contest, to which the owners of the *America* have challenged the yachtsmen of England, and which Mr. R. Stephenson, the eminent engineer, has accepted, by backing his own schooner, the *Titania*, against the *America*.

PAINE-BURGESS TESTIMONIAL.

"Among the visitors on Friday were many strangers,— Frenchmen *en route* for Havre, Germans in quiet wonderment at the excitement around them, and Americans already triumphing in the anticipated success of their countrymen. The cards containing the names and colors of the yachts described the course merely as being 'round the Isle of Wight;' the printed programme stated that it was to be 'round the Isle of Wight, inside Norman's Buoy and Sandhead Buoy, and outside the Nab.' The distinction gave rise, at the close of the race, to questioning the *America's* right to the Cup, as she did not sail outside the Nab Light; but this objection was not persisted in, and the Messrs. Stevens were presented with the Cup. The following yachts were entered. They were moored in a double line. No time allowed for tonnage: —

NAME.	CLASS.	TONS.	OWNERS.
"Beatrice	Schooner	161	Sir W. P. Carew.
Volante	Cutter	48	Mr. J. L. Cragie.
Arrow	Cutter	84	Mr. T. Chamberlayne.
Wyvern	Schooner	205	The Duke of Marlborough.
Ione	Schooner	75	Mr. A. Hill.
Constance	Schooner	218	The Marquis of Conyngham.
Titania	Schooner	100	Mr. R. Stephenson.
Gipsy Queen	Schooner	160	Sir H. B. Hoghton.
Alarm	Cutter	193	Mr. J. Weld.
Mona	Cutter	82	Lord A. Paget.
America	Schooner	170	Mr. J. B. Stevens, etc.
Brilliant	3-mast-schooner	392	Mr. G. H. Ackers.
Bacchante	Cutter	80	Mr. B. H. Jones.

NAME.	CLASS.	TONS.	OWNERS.
Freak . .	. Cutter .	60	Mr. W. Curling.
Stella . .	. Cutter .	65	Mr. R. Frankland.
Eclipse .	. Cutter . .	. 50	Mr. H. S. Fearon.
Fernande .	. Schooner . .	. 127	Major Martyn.
Aurora	. Cutter . .	. 47	Mr. T. Le Merchant.

"At 9.55 the preparatory gun was fired from the Clubhouse battery, and the yachts were soon sheeted from deck to topmast with clouds of canvas, huge gaff-topsails and balloon-jibs being greatly in vogue, and the *America* evincing her disposition to take advantage of her new jib by hoisting it with all alacrity. The whole flotilla not in the race were already in motion, many of them stretching down towards Osborne and Ryde to get good start of the clippers. Of the list above given the *Titania* and the *Stella* did not start, and the *Fernande* did not take her station (the latter was twice winner in 1850, and once this year; the *Stella* won once last year). Thus only fifteen started, of which seven were schooners, including the *Brilliant* (three-masted schooner), and eight were cutters. At 10 o'clock the signal gun for sailing was fired, and before the smoke had well cleared away the whole of the beautiful fleet was under weigh, moving steadily to the east with the tide and a gentle breeze. The start was effected splendidly, the yachts breaking away like a field of race-horses; the only laggard was the *America*, which did not move for a second or so after the others. Steamers, shore-boats, and yachts of all sizes buzzed along on each side of the course, and spread away for miles over the rippling sea — a sight such as the Adriatic never beheld in all the pride of Venice; such, beaten though we are, as no other country in the world could exhibit; while it is confessed that anything like it was never seen, even here, in the annals of yachting. Soon after they started a steamer went off from the roads, with the members of the sailing committee, Sir B. Graham, Bart., Commodore, Royal Yacht Squadron, and the following gentlemen: Lord Exmouth, Captain Lyon, Mr. A. Fontaine, Captain Ponsonby, Captain Corry, Messrs. Harvey, Leslie, Greg, and Reynolds. The American Minister, Mr. Abbott Lawrence, and his son, Col. Lawrence, *attaché* to the American Legation, arrived too late for the sailing of the *America*, but were accommodated on board the steamer, and went round the island in her; and several steamers, chartered by private gentlemen or for excursion trips, also accompanied the match.

"The *Gipsy Queen*, with all her canvas set, and in the strength of the tide, took the lead after starting, with the *Beatrice* next, and then, with little difference in order, the *Volante*, *Constance*, *Arrow*, and a flock of others. The *America* went easily for some time under mainsail (with a small gaff-top-sail of a triangular shape, braced up to the truck of the short and slender stick which serves as her maintop-mast), foresail, forestay-sail, and jib; while her opponents had every cloth set that the Club regulations allow. She soon began to creep upon them, passing some of the cutters to the windward. In a quarter of an hour she had left them all behind, except the *Constance*, *Beatrice*, and *Gipsy Queen*, which were well together, and went along smartly with the light breeze. The yachts were timed off No Man's Land buoy, and the character of the race at this moment may be guessed from the result:—

	H.	M.	S.
"Volante	11	7	0
Freak . .	11	8	20
Aurora . .	11	8	30
Gipsy Queen .	11	8	45
America	11	9	0
Beatrice	11	9	15
Alarm	11	9	20
Arrow . .	11	10	0
Bacchante .	11	10	15

"The other six were staggering about in the rear, and the *Wyvern* soon afterwards hauled her wind, and went back towards Cowes.

"The *America* speedily advanced to the front and got clear away from the rest. Off Sandown Bay, the wind freshening, she carried away her jib-boom; but, as she was well handled, the mishap produced no ill effect, and, during a lull which came on in the breeze for some time subsequently, her competitors gained a trifling advantage, but did not approach her. Off Ventnor the *America* was more than a mile ahead of the *Aurora*, then the nearest of the racing squadron; and hereabouts the number of her competitors was lessened by three cutters, the *Volante* having sprung her bowsprit, the *Arrow* having gone ashore, and the *Alarm* having staid by the *Arrow* to assist in getting her off. But from the moment the *America* had rounded St. Catherine's point, with a moderate breeze at S.S.W., the chances of coming up with her again were over. The *Wildfire*, which, though not in the match, kept up with the stranger for some time, was soon shaken off, and of the vessels in the match, the *Aurora* was the last that kept her in sight, until, the weather thickening, even that small comfort was lost to her. As the *America* approached the Needles, the wind fell, and a haze came on, not thick enough, however, to be very dangerous; and here she met and passed (saluting with her flag) the *Victoria and Albert* Royal yacht, with Her Majesty on board. Her Majesty waited for the *Aurora*, and then returned to Osborne, passing the *America* again in the Solent. About six o'clock, the *Aurora* being some five or six miles astern, and the result of the race inevitable, the steamers that had accompanied the yachts bore away for Cowes, where they landed their passengers. The evening fell darkly, heavy clouds being piled along the northern shore of the strait; and the thousands who had for hours lined the southern shore, from West Cowes long past the Castle, awaiting anxiously the appearance of the winner, and eagerly drinking in every rumour as to the progress of the match, were beginning to disperse, when the peculiar rig of the clipper was discerned through the gloom, and at 8h. 34m. o'clock (railway time, 8h. 37m., according to the secretary of the Royal Yacht Squadron) a gun from the flag-ship announced her arrival as the winner of the cup. The *Aurora* was announced at 8h. 58m.; the *Bacchante* at 9h. 30m.; the *Eclipse* at 9h. 45m.; the *Brilliant* at 1h. 20m. (Saturday morning). No account of the rest."

YACHT AMERICA, 1851.
FROM THE LONDON ILLUSTRATED NEWS.

It will be seen by this account that the prize so won was the Yacht Squadron's Cup, and not the Queen's Cup, offered a day or two later, for which the *America* did not contest, owing to light winds.

On Saturday evening the *America* sailed from Cowes to Osborne, on the intimation that the Queen wished to inspect her. On the arrival there Her Majesty, with Prince Albert and suite, went on board and spent half an hour in a close inspection of the famous boat. On Monday, a race took place at Ryde for a splendid cup presented by the Queen, in the expectation that the *America* would contest. In consequence of there not being at least a six-knot breeze, the *America* did not start. But, as the *News* stated, "Just before the vessels got in, the raking *America* was seen making her way round the Nab Light, and, with a most extraordinary movement, made one reach from the Light to Stroke Bay, and by another tack, rounded the *Brilliant* in gallant style. To accomplish the same feat that the *America* had performed, the *Alarm* took ten tacks, and the *Volante* at least twenty for the same distance. Had the *America*, therefore, proceeded into the match at the appointed hour, there can be no doubt that the same fortunate result would have greeted her as at Cowes last week."

This closed the *America's* record in British waters, and she returned to New York the unquestioned champion of the world.[1] The trophy which she had captured has

---

[1] Commodore Stevens sold the *America* to Lord De Blanquiere. Her English owner altered her rig somewhat, cut down her masts, and used her for cruising until 1861, when her name was changed to the *Camilla*. Then an American gentleman purchased her as a Confederate cruiser, put a heavy gun on her, and

ever since been rightfully known as the America's Cup, and we have obtained a careful delineation of it. The original source of the prize ceases to be of any importance, since, by the subsequent acts of its owners, it has become the highest prize now offered to the ambition of skilful designers of racing yachts and of competent owners and sailors of such crafts.

As has been said of the Derby, it is the "Blue Ribbon" of yachting, and as such, it will undoubtedly continue for years to stimulate the skill and enterprise of the two greatest maritime nations.

The owners of the *America*, Messrs. J. C. Stevens, Edwin A. Stevens, Hamilton Wilkes, J. Beckman Finley, and George L. Schuyler, kept possession of the cup until

---

named her the *Memphis*. He soon discovered that, though in a good wind she could beat most of the steamers even, in a light wind she was no match for the slowest vessel in the Northern blockading fleet. Thereupon he took her up the St. John's river, Florida, and sank her in the mud for safety, where she remained for several months. She was then dug out and sent by the American frigate *Wabash* to New York, whence she was taken to Annapolis, and nominally used as a training schooner for the cadets. Afterwards she was carried to New York, and refitted at an expense of $25,000, to sail in the race against the *Livonia*, an English yacht which came over here to contest the possession of the America's Cup. Being fitted up like a man-of-war, and sailed by a man who knew nothing of yachting, she came in third at that race.

In 1871 she was sold at auction, and bought by Gen. Benjamin F. Butler and Col. Jonas H. French. She was then put in her present condition. In 1875 she sailed an ocean race at the Isles of Shoals against the *Resolute*, a fast New York yacht, where she won successively two races. In 1876 she sailed in the International Race at the Centennial Exposition, where she won an easy victory. Afterward, when the Canadian yacht, *Countess of Dufferin*, came here to contest the cup, the *America*, not belonging to the New York Yacht Club, was not allowed to take part in the race; but, though not in racing trim, she crossed the starting line after both boats, and beat them in a twenty-mile stretch to windward. Such is a brief history of the winner of the America's Cup.

July 8, 1857, when they offered it to the New York Yacht Club, subject to the following conditions: —

"Any organized yacht club of any foreign country shall always be entitled, through any one or more of its members, to claim the right of sailing a match for this Cup with any yacht or other vessel of not less than thirty or more than three hundred tons, measured by the custom-house rule of the country to which the vessel belongs.

"The parties desiring to sail for the Cup may make any match with the yacht club in possession of the same that may be determined upon by mutual consent; but, in case of disagreement as to terms, the match shall be sailed over the usual course for the annual regatta of the yacht club in possession of the Cup, and subject to its rules and sailing regulations — the challenging party being bound to give six months' notice in writing, fixing the day they wish to start. This notice to embrace the length, custom-house measurement, rig and name of the vessel.

"It is to be distinctly understood, that the Cup is to be the property of the club, and not of the members thereof, or owners of the vessel winning it in a match; and that the condition of keeping it open to be sailed for by yacht clubs of all foreign countries upon the terms above laid down, shall forever attach to it, thus making it perpetually a Challenge Cup for friendly competition between foreign countries."

For eleven years no attempt was made to challenge the possession of the Cup, but in October, 1868, Mr. James Ashbury, the owner of the English schooner-yacht *Cambria*, opened a correspondence with the New York Yacht

Club. Nothing came of this attempt during 1869; but, in 1870, Mr. Ashbury brought over the *Cambria*, and a race for the Cup was sailed in New York harbor, August 8, 1870.

The *Cambria* was built by Ratsey, of Cowes, Isle of Wight, in 1868, and was 248 tons New York measurement, or 128 tons Royal Thames Yacht Club measurement. Her dimensions were: —

Length (from stem to sternpost), 108 feet; beam, 21 feet; depth of hold, 11 feet; draught of water, 12 feet; mainmast (hounds to deck), 61 feet; foremast, 56 feet 6 inches; main-boom, 61 feet; main-gaff, 33 feet 9 inches; fore-gaff, 25; bowsprit outboard, 35 feet; maintop-mast, 35 feet 6 inches; foretop-mast, 32 feet 3 inches; maintop-sail yard, 32 feet; foretop-sail yard, 29 feet.

FIRST INTERNATIONAL RACE, NEW YORK, AUGUST 8, 1870.

Under the terms of the trust, this race was open to all the fleet (being the same conditions under which the *America* won the Cup), although Mr. Ashbury protested against the decision.

The following table gives the result. Only schooners entered, and those marked with an asterisk were keel-boats.

Schooners. Start, 11 : 26 : 00 A.M.

NAME.	FINISH.	ELAPSED TIME.	CORRECTED TIME.
	H. M. S.	H. M. S.	H. M. S.
Magic . .	3 33 54	4 07 54	3 58 26.2
Idler . .	3 37 23	4 11 23	4 09 35.1
Silvie . . .	3 55 12	4 29 12	4 23 45.3

PAINE-BURGESS TESTIMONIAL.　21

NAME.	FINISH.	ELAPSED TIME.	CORRECTED TIME.
	H. M. S.	H. M. S.	H. M. S.
*America	3 47 54	4 21 54	4 23 51.4
*Dauntless	3 35 28½	4 09 23½	4 29 19.2
Madgie	3 55 07	4 29 07	4 29 57.1
Phantom	3 55 05	4 29 05	4 30 44.5
Alice	4 18 27½	4 52 27½	4 34 15.2
Halcyon	4 03 08	4 37 08	4 00 35.9
*Cambria	4 00 57	4 34 57	4 37 38.9
Calypso	4 15 29	4 49 29	4 40 21.3
*Fleetwing	4 02 09½	4 36 19½	4 41 20.5
Madelaine	4 14 46	4 48 46	4 42 35.4
*Tarolinta	4 10 23	4 44 23	4 47 29.2
*Rambler	4 51 35½	4 51 35½	4 48 35.5

It will be seen that the race was won by the *Magic*, a yacht much smaller than most of her competitors. By the table of entries in 1871, giving cubical contents for measurement, we find *Magic*, 2,492 feet; *Idler*, 2,932 feet; *Dauntless*, 7,124 feet; *Sappho*, 7,431 feet; *Rambler*, 5,909 feet.

The race was, however, a finality for that year, and the little *Magic* stands first on the list of defenders of the Cup, as the *Cambria*[1] does on the roll of its assailants.

---

[1] It may be noted that in 1870 the New York yacht *Sappho* was sent to England, and there raced with the *Cambria*, winning the first race, May 10. On the second race Mr. Ashbury refused to sail, and the *Sappho* went over the course alone. The third race was also won by the *Sappho*. Then the *Cambria* raced the *Dauntless* from Gaunt Head, Ireland, to Sandy Hook Lightship, and the English boat won by 1 hour and 17 minutes. After the America's Cup race the *Cambria* sailed in various matches here, but was beaten by the *Palmer*, the *Sappho*, and the *Dauntless*.

SECOND INTERNATIONAL RACE, 1871.

Mr. Ashbury, after his experience with the *Cambria*, resolved to build another yacht and to challenge again the defenders of the America's Cup. In the spring and summer of 1871 he had an extensive correspondence with the officers of the New York Yacht Club, complaining especially of their former decision, by which a challenger was obliged to sail against tne whole fleet. After considerable discussion, and with the approval of Mr. George L. Schuyler, the only survivor of the donors of the Cup, the Club decided that they would "sail one or more representative vessels against the same number of foreign challenging vessels." Then Mr. Ashbury claimed that, as he belonged to twelve different British yacht clubs, he was entitled to a separate race for and in behalf of each club, and that, if he won a single race, the Cup was to be awarded to the club which he represented on that day.

This the New York Club considered as inadmissible under the deed of trust controlling the Cup; but it was finally agreed that there should be seven races sailed between Oct. 16 and Oct. 25, — three over the New York Club course, and four over a course of twenty miles to windward beyond Sandy Hook Lightship and back.

Mr. Ashbury's new yacht was the *Livonia*, and the New York Club named the keel-schooners *Sappho* and *Dauntless*, and the centre-board schooners *Columbia* and *Palmer*, reserving the right to name one of these as the competitor of the *Livonia* on the morning of each race.

The *Livonia's* dimensions were as follows: Tonnage, 280 tons, old measurement; tonnage for racing, 264 tons; length between perpendiculars, 115 feet 2 inches; beam, 23 feet 7 inches; draught, 12 feet 6 inches; length of mainmast from hounds to deck, 68 feet; foremast, 64 feet.

The first and second races were won by the *Columbia*, the inside course by 27 minutes and 4 seconds; the outside by about 7 minutes. The third race was won by the *Livonia*, by 15 minutes and 10 seconds, owing to accidents to her competitor.

The fourth and fifth races were won by the *Sappho*, respectively by 30 minutes and 21 seconds, and 25 minutes and 27 seconds.

The second race was claimed by Mr. Ashbury on technical grounds, which were disallowed by the Club; and the contest closed with the American boats winning four out of the first five races, and thereby closing the series of seven. Much bad feeling was caused by Mr. Ashbury's claims and protests; but had he been allowed to call the second race a draw, there is no probability that his position would have been improved, as the *Livonia* was also beaten in October by the *Dauntless*.

THIRD INTERNATIONAL RACE, 1876.

After an interval of five years a new competitor presented himself for the America's Cup. This was Mr. Charles Gifford, of the Royal Canadian Yacht Club, who named the *Countess of Dufferin* as the challenging vessel. As usual the challenge asked for some modification of the rules of the New York Club. We have seen that the trust deed provided strictly for one race only, open to the whole fleet. The holders of the America's Cup had already limited their defence to one vessel for each race, and now, after some correspondence, they further conceded that the challenging yacht should sail against only one opponent, to be named in advance, to sail all the races. Moreover, as many yachtsmen considered the New York Club's inside course to be a bad one for a stranger, the Club decided to sail three races, — one inside, one outside, and the third, if required, to be decided by lot.

The *Countess of Dufferin* is described as 221 tons register, 107 feet over all, 24 feet beam, and 6½ feet draught. Her official certificate of measurement, from the Secretary of the Royal Canadian Yacht Club, stated her length at 91 feet 6 inches; beam, 23 feet 6 inches; and her tonnage at 200 tons. Her mainmast was 65 feet, and her topmast 30 feet long, with a main-boom 55 feet in length. It was conceded that the Canadian boat was built upon the model of our own boats, and, as the result proved, she was only a rough copy at that. The New York Club selected as its champion the *Madelaine*, built as a sloop in 1868, afterwards lengthened, and a second mast added. She was at this time owned by Com. Jacob Voorhis, Jr.

The measurement at the first race gave *Countess* 95.53 feet water-line; 9,028.04 cubic feet, contents. *Madelaine*, 95.02 feet water-line; 8,499.17 cubic feet, contents.

The first race, over the inside course, was sailed August 11, and the *Madelaine* won by 9 minutes 58 seconds actual time, and 10 minutes 59 seconds corrected time. The second race, twenty miles to windward from Sandy Hook and return, was sailed August 12, and the *Madelaine* again won, by 27 minutes 14 seconds corrected time. The *America* sailed over the course at the same time, and beat the Canadian yacht by 19 minutes and 9 seconds. Even these figures fail to give the real inferiority of the challenging boat, as she was overmatched in every respect.

Another period of five years elapsed before American yachtsmen were called upon to defend the Cup. Capt. Alexander Cuthbert, of Belleville, Ont., was the real projector of the previous Canadian attempt, and in 1881 he built the sloop-yacht *Atlanta* for the purpose of again trying his luck. A challenge was made in his behalf by the Bay of Quinte Yacht Club, of Belleville, of which he was a member. The New York Yacht Club, as usual, waived the six months' notice required by the rules, and proceeded to select a champion from their own boats. After various trials the *Mischief* was chosen to defend the Cup.

FOURTH INTERNATIONAL RACE, 1881.

The *Atlanta* varied the monotony of the previous attempts by arriving in New York *via* the Erie Canal. She was about forty-five tons, and measured 70 feet 1 inch over all; 62 feet 10 inches on the water line; 19 feet beam; 6 feet 10 inches depth of hold. She drew 5 feet 6 inches aft, and 3 feet 6 inches forward, and with board down, 16 feet 6 inches. Her spars were a 70-foot mast, 34-foot top-mast, 25-foot bowsprit, outboard, 70-foot boom, and 36-foot gaff.

The *Mischief* was considered at the time the best boat in the fleet, though the *Gracie* was but little inferior; and each, as the result proved, was abundantly able to protect the Cup.

The first race was assigned for November 8, the Canadian being unable to appear earlier; but was not sailed on that day, owing to there being so little wind that there was no probability of making the race in the stipulated time of eight hours. It was sailed, however, on November 9, the *Mischief* beating the *Atlanta* by 28 minutes and 30¼ seconds, corrected time, while the *Gracie* also beat the *Mischief* by 6 minutes 27 seconds, corrected time.

The second and final race was sailed November 10, the course being sixteen miles to leeward from buoy No. 5, and return. The *Mischief* beat the *Atlanta* 38 minutes 54 seconds, and the *Gracie* beat the Canadian 34 minutes 16 seconds, the *Mischief* also beating the *Gracie*.

The victory was so easy as to render the race a farce. The Canadian boat was evidently pitted against antagonists entirely beyond her strength, and the success won was a poor recompense for the trouble and expense to which the defenders of the Cup had been put.

The Cup was accordingly surrendered to the survivor of the donors and regranted on new conditions, as set forth in the following papers: —

NEW YORK, January 4, 1882.

To the Secretary of the New York Yacht Club: —

DEAR SIR, — I have to acknowledge the receipt of your letter of Dec. 17, 1881, enclosing the resolutions of the New York

Yacht Club of that date, and also the return of the America's Cup to me as the survivor of the original donors.

I fully concur with the views expressed in the resolutions, that the deed of gift made so many years ago is, under present circumstances, inadequate to meet the intentions of the donors, and too onerous upon the club in possession, which is required to defend it against all challengers.

As the New York Yacht Club, by your communication and under the resolutions themselves, express a desire to be again placed in possession of the Cup under new conditions, I have conferred with the committee appointed at the meeting, and have prepared a new deed of gift of this Cup as a perpetual Challenge Cup. It is hoped that, as regards both challenging and challenged parties, its terms will be considered just and satisfactory to organized Yacht Clubs of all countries.

There is one clause which may require explanation. Owing to the present and increasing size of ocean steamers it would be quite feasible for an American, English, or French Club to transport on their decks yachts of large tonnage. This might be availed of in such a way that the match would not be a test of sea-going qualities as well as of speed, which would essentially detract from the interest of a national competition.

The America's Cup is again offered to the New York Yacht Club, subject to the following conditions: —

Any organized Yacht Club of a foreign country, incorporated, patented, or licensed by the Legislature, admiralty or other executive department, having for its annual regatta an ocean water-course on the sea or on an arm of the sea (or one which combines both), practicable for vessels of 300 tons, shall always be entitled, through one or more of its members, to the right of sailing a match for this Cup, with a yacht or other vessel propelled by sails only, and constructed in the country to which the Challenging Club belongs, against any one yacht or vessel as aforesaid, constructed in the country of the club holding the Cup.

The yacht or vessel to be of not less than 30 or more than 300 tons, measured by the Custom-House rule in use by the country of the challenging party.

The challenging party shall give six months' notice in writing, naming the day for the proposed race, which day shall not be less than seven months from the date of the notice.

The parties intending to sail for the Cup may, by mutual consent, make any arrangement satisfactory to both as to the date, course, time allowance, number of trials, rules, and sailing regulations, and any and all other conditions of the match, in which case also the six months' notice may be waived.

In case the parties cannot mutually agree upon the terms of a match, then the challenging party shall have the right to contest for the Cup in one trial, sailed over the usual course of the Annual Regatta of the club holding the Cup, subject to its rules and sailing regulations, the challenged party not being required to name its representative until the time agreed upon for the start.

Accompanying the six months' notice there must be a Custom-House certificate of the measurement, and a statement of the dimensions, rig, and name of the vessel.

No vessel which has been defeated in a match for this Cup can be again selected by any club for its representative until after a contest for it by some other vessel has intervened, or until after the expiration of two years from the time such contest has taken place.

Vessels intending to compete for this Cup must proceed under sail on their own bottoms to the port where the contest is to take place.

Should the club holding the Cup be for any cause dissolved, the Cup shall be handed over to any club of the same nationality it may select which comes under the foregoing rules.

It is to be distinctly understood that the Cup is to be the property of the club, and not of the owners of the vessel winning it in a match, and that the condition of keeping it open to be sailed for by organized Yacht Clubs of all foreign countries, upon the terms above laid down, shall forever attach to it, thus making it perpetually a Challenge Cup for friendly competition between foreign countries.

GEORGE L. SCHUYLER.

A copy of this communication was sent to all foreign yacht clubs, accompanied by the following letter from the Secretary of the New York Club: —

The New York Yacht Club, having accepted the gift, with the conditions above expressed, consider this a fitting occasion to present the subject to the Yacht Clubs of all nations, and invoke from them a spirited contest for the championship, and trust that it may be the source of continued friendly strife between the institutions of this description throughout the world, and therefore request that this communication may be laid before your members at their earliest meeting, and earnestly invite a friendly competition for the possession of the prize, tendering to any gentleman who may favor us with a visit, and who may enter into the contest, a liberal, hearty welcome, and the strictest fair play.

CHARLES A. MINTON,
Secretary New York Yacht Club.

THE CHALLENGE OF THE GENESTA.

Mr. J. Beavor-Webb, an English yacht designer of note, took the initiatory steps toward the international struggle for the America's Cup in 1885. In a letter, which was received on Dec. 29, 1884, he notified the New York Yacht Club of challenges for the America's Cup, from Sir Richard Sutton, Bart., owner of the English cutter *Genesta*, and from Lieut. William R. Henn, R.N., owner of the English cutter *Galatea*, which was then in process of construction. At a meeting of the Club, held on Feb. 26, 1885, Mr. Beavor-Webb's formal challenges, cabled on that day, were accepted, and were as follows: —

18 CRANBY GARDENS, S.W.,
LONDON, Feb. 26, 1885.

To CHARLES MINTON, *Secretary of the New York Yacht Club:* —

DEAR SIR, — Referring to my letter of the 6th of December last, I now beg to challenge, on behalf of Sir Richard Sutton, Bart., and Lieutenant Henn, R.N., for the America Cup, in accordance with Mr. Schuyler's letter of 4th of January, 1882, embodied in your letter of 15th of February, 1882. Sir Richard Sutton challenges on behalf of the Royal Yacht Squadron, of which he is a member, and Lieutenant Henn on behalf of the Royal Northern Yacht Club, of which he is a member. The regatta courses of both these clubs are on the sea or upon the arms of the sea, and are practicable for yachts of 300 tons. I inclose letters from the Secretaries of the Royal Yacht Squadron and the Royal Northern Yacht Club, authorizing Sir Richard Sutton, Bart., and Lieutenant Henn, R.N., to challenge as representing these clubs.

Sir Richard Sutton's *Genesta* is cutter-rigged, and her dimensions are: length on load water-line, 81 feet; beam, 15 feet; depth moulded, 11.75. Her tonnage, according to the Yacht Racing Association rules, is 80 tons. It is not possible to comply literally with paragraph 11 of the conditions, as there is no such thing in this country as a Custom-house certificate of measurement, but I inclose a certified extract from the ship's register, in which her dimensions and tonnage are stated. The register itself, being the title to the vessel, obviously cannot be sent. The *Genesta's* dimensions are also given in Lloyd's Yacht Register for 1884, which register is deemed official.

Lieut. Henn's yacht, the *Galatea*, is to be cutter-rigged. Her dimensions are: length on the load water-line, 86.80 feet; beam, 15 feet; draught extreme, 13.50; depth moulded in figures, blank copy. A certified copy of her dimensions is inclosed. It is intended that Sir Richard Sutton's challenge shall take priority of Lieut. Henn's challenge. Therefore, if Sir Richard Sutton's yacht is fortunate enough to win the Cup, Lieut. Henn's challenge, under the conditions of the contest paragraph, necessarily falls to the ground; but, should Sir Richard Sutton's cutter be beaten, it is proposed that the match with Lieut. Henn's vessel shall take place as soon as practicable after those with Sir Richard Sutton's vessel. It is further proposed that the matches with the *Genesta* shall be sailed between the 20th of August and September 1, and those with the *Galatea* before September 17, the latter date being within seven months of the date of this letter, as required by the eighth paragraph of the conditions. It is also proposed that each match shall consist of three races over the same course, sailed on different days, with at least one intervening day, either yacht winning two out of the three races to be the winner. As it was the intention of the donors of the cup, as expressed in Mr. Schuyler's letter of January 4, 1882, that the contest for its possession should be sailed over an open sea-course, it is the wish of the challengers that an ocean course should be selected, free, so far as practicable, from all complications as to tides and shallow water. The challengers further suggest that the time allowance between the competing yachts should be the mean of the time ascertained by the New York Yacht Club, and the

Yacht Racing Association rules of measurement and time allowances.

It is very important that the details of the races should be settled under the ninth paragraph of the conditions, because in the following paragraphs there is a condition which might give advantage to the holders of the Cup, namely, the condition which would enable them to name their representative at the time of the start, and then to select their vessel according to the weather. The challengers themselves do not attach much importance to this condition, but it is obviously desirable to avoid anything in such contests which might have the appearance of giving the advantage to one side. The challengers therefore respectfully suggest, for the purpose of settling the details referred to in paragraph nine, that each party should name a representative, with a referee mutually chosen. The challengers think that Mr. G. L. Schuyler, the surviving donor of the Cup, would be the most appropriate person, if he would undertake the office, to act as referee; and, if this suggestion meets with the concurrence of the members of the New York Yacht Club, the challengers name J. M. Woodbury, Fleet Surgeon of the Seawanhaka Yacht Club, as their representative.

In conclusion, I am to add that the challengers, desiring that these contests should be a true test between the American and English types of yacht, will do everything in their power to insure that result, and they feel satisfied that their views will be fully appreciated and reciprocated by the members of the New York Yacht Club.

I shall be happy to furnish any information that may be required. I remain, dear sir, for Sir Richard Sutton, Bart., and Lieut. Henn, R.N., yours faithfully,

J. BEAVOR-WEBB.

The following committee were given entire charge of the details for the races: Philip Schuyler, J. F. Tams, C.

PURITAN.

H. Stebbins, Jules A. Montant, Joseph R. Busk, and Vice-Com. George L. Schuyler.

It was decided that there should be two, and if necessary three, races, — one over the regular New York Yacht Club course; distance, 38 miles; one over a triangular course of 40 miles, outside of Sandy Hook, N.J.; and one over a forty-mile course (twenty miles to windward and twenty miles to leeward) off Sandy Hook. The limit of time for sailing each race was fixed at seven hours, and provision was made for accident. The measurement rules of the New York Yacht Club were adopted, and it was agreed that the Cup defender should be named at least one week prior to the first race.

The method of obtaining the racing length of the yachts was as follows: —

$$\frac{2 \times \text{water-line length} + \sqrt{\text{sail area}}}{3}$$

THE BOSTON SLOOP *PURITAN*.

In the early part of 1885, five gentlemen, members of the Eastern Yacht Club, consisting of Vice-Com. J. Malcolm Forbes, Gen. Charles J. Paine, Mr. Edward Burgess, Secretary, Mr. William Gray, Jr., and Mr. Francis H. Peabody, met at the office of Mr. Forbes to discuss matters appertaining to the Club. Allusion to the challenge of the *Genesta* was there made, and, after a discussion of the relative types of English and American yachts, it was agreed that none of the latter possessed the speed necessary to successfully defend the challenge. Mr. Peabody having withdrawn, the other gentlemen continued the conversation until the enthusiasm increased to the point of suggesting the building of an Eastern boat which would combine all the recent ideas in American yacht designing. The suggestion met with hearty approval, and plans were then made to secure the coöperation of other yachtsmen, the syndicate to assume the entire cost of designing, building, and fitting out the new boat. At a subsequent meeting the syndicate was formed, the members being Gen. Charles J. Paine, Vice-Com. J. Malcolm Forbes, Mr. William Gray, Jr., Com. Henry S. Hovey, Rear-Com. William F. Weld, Mr. Augustus Hemenway, Mr. W. H. Forbes, Mr. John L. Gardner, Mr. J. Montgomery Sears, Mr. F. L. Higginson, and one other, who desired that his name be not made public. The stock was divided into ten shares, one being divided between Messrs. Sears and Higginson. The entire responsibility of designing, building, and sailing the yacht was placed with Messrs. Forbes, Paine, and Gray, the former being chosen chairman of the committee. In their subsequent consultations the committee sought the advice of Mr. Edward Burgess, in whose ideas they had much faith. About this time it was learned that Messrs. James Gordon Bennett and W. P. Douglas, of the New York Yacht Club, had undertaken the building of an iron sloop, which was afterward named the *Priscilla*, to compete for the same honors. The Boston gentlemen, urged on by this intelligence, exerted themselves to combine in the Boston sloop the very best ideas obtainable, and, after a frequent exchange of views, Mr. Burgess handed to them the designs of a yacht which eventually brought renown to her designer, her owners, and to the city of Boston.

Messrs. George Lawley & Sons, of South Boston, secured the contract for the construction, and when the sloop left their hands their work was declared to have been well and faithfully performed. The keel was laid in March, and the new sloop, christened *Puritan*, was launched on May 26, 1885. The name was given by Mr. Forbes, and her coat of white, symbolic of purity, corresponded with the name. The rigging and fitting-out progressed rapidly, under the supervision of the committee.

The *Puritan* is a centre-board yacht, and built entirely of wood. Her keel was shaped from an oak stick, 56 feet long and 26 inches square. The lead keel is 45 feet long, 2 feet wide, and 16 inches deep. The frames are of the best white oak, spaced 22 inches on the centres. The centre-board, of hard pine, with upper and lower planks of oak, is 22 feet long, 11 feet deep, and 4 inches thick. The five lower strakes of the hull are of oak and are copper-fastened. Above the water-line the planking is of hard pine, $2\frac{3}{4}$ inches thick. On the deck, which is flush, the planking is of white pine, and runs the entire length of the yacht.

Her frames are double, except those about the stern-post and stem. The rudder-head is of locust, 10 inches in diameter; the backing is of oak, and tapers to $2\frac{1}{2}$ inches. The after-companion-way is 5×3 feet, and the forward one 3 feet square, and they, with the sky-lights, are of mahogany. Hackmatack was used for the twelve pairs of hanging knees, and yellow pine, 8×10 at the mast and $6\frac{1}{2}$ and $5\frac{1}{2}$ inches for the others, was used for the deck beams. The step of the mast is made of iron, which weighs 1,000 pounds, and is strongly bolted to the keel. Attached to the lower plank of the centreboard is an iron shoe weighing 900 pounds, and having a knife edge. The stanchions are made of locust, 16 inches forward and 14 inches aft, and the rail is of oak. The interior finishing and furnishing are of the best. The main cabin, 16×12 feet, is finished in mahogany and pine, and has two mahogany sideboards, large lounges, and mahogany posts carved to resemble ships' cables. The ladies' cabin, abaft the main saloon, is beautifully furnished and has every convenience. Two state-rooms, $10\frac{1}{2} \times 6\frac{1}{2}$ feet, are forward of the cabin, and just forward of these is a lavatory. There is a room for the captain, two for the mates, a roomy galley, and a forecastle with iron swinging-berths, which will accommodate eighteen men. Crucible steel wire was used for the rigging. Messrs. H. Pigeon & Sons, of East Boston, furnished the spars, and Messrs. J. H. McManus & Son, of Boston, the sails, which are of Plymouth duck.

The maiden trip of the *Puritan* was made on the 17th of June, 1885, only, however, for the purpose of stretching her sails, and not to test her speed. On this occasion, as on all others during that season, she was under the command of Capt. Aubrey Crocker, of Cohasset, Mass., who was an adept at yacht sailing, and had attracted the attention of the *Puritan's* owners by his skilful handling of the sloop *Shadow*, in which he won many victories. The trial trip of the *Puritan* was made on June 20, 1885, and on this and subsequent trials the result was most gratifying. On the 30th of June she was entered for her first race, in the regatta of the Eastern Yacht

GENESTA.

Club, off Marblehead; and over a triangular course of 30 miles she led the fleet, and easily defeated the fastest Eastern sloops and schooners. She showed remarkable speed during the cruise of the New York Yacht Club in July, and on August 3 she won the Goelet Cup, off Newport, R.I., defeating not only the crack yachts *Bedouin*, *Gracie*, *Mohican*, *Fortuna*, and *Montauk*, but the New York sloop *Priscilla*, which had been built to contend with her for the honor of sailing for the America's Cup in September. With slight alterations in her ballast and main-boom she was ready to enter the contest which should decide which American sloop would be named to sail with the *Genesta* for the international trophy. Her official measurements, as given by her designer, were as follows: —

Length over all, 94 feet; length on water-line, 81 feet 1½ inches; beam, 22 feet 7 inches; draught, 8 feet 8 inches; length of mast, from deck to hounds, 60 feet; length of top-mast, 44 feet; length of main-boom, 76 feet 6 inches; length of gaff, 47 feet; length of bowsprit, outboard, 38 feet; length of spinnaker boom, 62 feet; displacement, 105 tons; ballast, 48 tons; sail area (New York Yacht Club rules), 7,982 square feet; racing measurement (New York Yacht Club rules), 83.85.

THE ENGLISH CUTTER *GENESTA*.

The English cutter *Genesta*, owned by Sir Richard Sutton, Bart., hailed from Glasgow, Scot., and was designed by Mr. J. Beavor-Webb, of England. Built in the best manner by Messrs. D. & W. Henderson, of Glasgow, Scot., at Partick, on the Clyde, in the winter of 1883-4, she was launched in April, 1884. Her owner is a gentleman of large fortune and an excellent reputation as a yachtsman, and in the *Genesta* every care was taken in construction and fitting to make her as perfect a boat as money could procure.

She is a typical English cutter, and a fine-looking vessel, and up to the year 1885 was, undoubtedly, the fastest English yacht ever sent to these shores. Her measurements, as given by her designer for this work, are as follows: —

Length over all, 96.40 feet; length on water-line, 81 feet; beam, 15 feet; draught, 13 feet; depth of hold, 11.75 feet; area of midship section, 103 feet; length of mast, from deck to hounds, 52 feet; length of top-mast, 47.50 feet; length of boom, 70 feet; length of gaff, 44 feet; length of bowsprit, outboard, 36.50 feet; length of spinnaker boom, 64 feet; displacement, 141 tons; total ballast, 72 tons; ballast on keel, 70 tons; sail area (New York Yacht Club rules), 7,150 square feet; racing measurement (New York Yacht Club rules), 83.50.

Her frame is of steel, and she is planked with oak. Keelson, stringers, and strengthening plates are all of steel, and she is steadied by a lead keel weighing 70 tons. The deck fittings present various novelties. The bowsprit, which is a reefing one, comes over the stem-head in the centre of the yacht, with more than the usual difficulties in the way of reefing it. To obviate this difficulty one of the cheeks of the steel bits is hinged. This device permits the bowsprit heel to be swung around clear of the scuttle and the capstan, and run aft alongside the mast. The fore-scuttle, oval in form, is a section of steel tube, around which the wire fall of the bobstay tackle is coiled in easier turn than it would be belayed in the ordinary way. In consequence of her deck fittings one feature is especially noticeable, — the appearance of light and elegance everywhere attained, and which adds to the available space for handling the yacht.

The *Genesta* has a fine cabin, fitted up lightly and elegantly, a ladies' cabin aft, and spacious accommodations for the captain, crew, and steward. The whole length of the yacht has been utilized, and the space obtained is remarkable. The hull is coppered to within a few feet of her covering board. Her rigging is of modern English style, with runners, runner pennants, and runner tackles to brace aft the mast, also preventer back-stays. She carries a main-sail, club and working top-sails, forestay-sail, jib, jib top-sail, balloon jibs, balloon-jib top-sail, and spinnaker, which were made by the famous English sail-maker, Lapthorne.

The *Genesta's* deck gains in length of look from the fineness of her ends, her counter being the narrowest and lightest seen on any cutter of the same size up to this time. The dead rise of the *Puritan* and *Genesta* differ greatly, the *Genesta* being wedge-shaped, while the *Puritan* has a fuller and more rounding hull. Her sailing-master, during her advent in American waters, was Capt. John Carter, who was a clever Clyde sailor of much experience in sailing racing-yachts.

The first race in which the *Genesta* took part was sailed on May 31, 1884, when she defeated the fast English yacht *Vanduara* by 2 minutes and 55 seconds, from Southend to Harwich. This victory was followed by numerous others; and she proved to be a boat of wonderful speed and reflected high credit on her designer. In thirty-four contests with the best English yachts she won seven first and ten second prizes. On her arrival on this side of the Atlantic, in the summer of 1885, she was thoroughly overhauled, preparatory to the Cup races, but her rig and ballast were not altered.

THE TRIAL RACES OF 1885.

The America's Cup committee of the New York Yacht Club having given notice that three trial races would be sailed by yachts, to be entered for the honor of defending America's title to the Cup, the first trial was set for Thursday, Aug. 20, 1885, the course being from the lightship *Wreck of Scotland*, off Sandy Hook, N.J., around a mark-boat stationed twenty miles to windward and back to the starting-point.

On that day, however, the wind was so light that a postponement was made, and the first race occurred on Friday, August 21.

The following yachts were entered: —

Puritan, centre-board sloop, Boston, racing measurement, 83.85; *Priscilla*, centre-board sloop, New York, racing measurement, 85.30; *Gracie*, centre-board sloop, New York, racing measurement, 71.62; *Bedouin*, cutter, New York, racing measurement, 71.45.

The wind at the start was blowing from the south at the rate of nine miles an hour, and when the whistle to send the boats off was blown, they all had their main-sails, working gaff-top-sails, and two jibs set. The *Puritan* and the *Priscilla* crossed the line together at 11 : 13 : 48, the *Gracie*, at 11 : 14 : 06, and the *Bedouin*, at 11 : 14 : 40 o'clock.

The interest in the race centred principally in the performances of the *Puritan* and *Priscilla*, owing to the general belief in the superiority of the new models, and because of the local pride exhibited respectively by the admirers of the Boston and the New York boats. The race was a fine one in every respect, and was well contested from start to finish, resulting in a decisive victory for the *Puritan*, which crossed the line fully two miles ahead of the *Priscilla*.

THE SUMMARY OF THE RACE.

Course. — 40 miles; 20 miles to windward and return.
Wind. — Average force about 9 knots, south.

	Start.	Outer Mark.	Finish.	Elapsed Time.	Corrected Time.
	H. M. S.	H. M. S.	H. M. S.	H. M. S.	H. M. S.
Puritan	11 13 48	2 28 00	4 12 07	4 58 19	4 57 05
Priscilla	11 13 48	2 40 37	4 22 05	5 08 17	5 08 17
Bedouin	11 14 40	2 52 15	4 40 09	5 25 29	5 15 51
Gracie	11 14 06	3 13 10	4 56 39	5 42 33	5 32 58

The *Puritan* defeated the *Priscilla* by 11 minutes 12 seconds; the *Bedouin*, by 18 minutes 46 seconds; the *Gracie*, by 35 minutes 53 seconds.

The *Priscilla* allowed the *Puritan* 1 minute 14 seconds; the *Bedouin*, 9 minutes 38 seconds; the *Gracie*, 9 minutes 35 seconds.

THE SECOND TRIAL RACE TOOK PLACE AUG. 22, 1885, over a triangular course of forty miles, beginning at the Scotland Lightship and running thirteen and one-third miles south-east by east, half east. The entries were the same as in the previous contest. The wind was south-west by south, and was light, with a fine rain falling. The *Puritan* crossed the line at 12 : 25 : 45 ; the *Priscilla*, at 12 : 26 : 27 ; the *Gracie* and *Bedouin*, 12 : 27 o'clock.

The *Priscilla* was more fortunate in this race, and succeeded in crossing the finish line a winner by 5 minutes 14 seconds, corrected time.

THE SUMMARY OF THE RACE.

COURSE. — 40 miles, over an equilateral triangle, starting from the Scotland Lightship.

WIND. — Light, south-west by south.

	Start.	First Mark.	Second Mark.	Finish.	Elapsed Time.	Corrected Time.
	H. M. S.	H. M. S.	H. M. S.	H. M. S.	H. M. S.	H. M. S.
Priscilla	12 26 27	2 16 05	5 30 54	6 32 53	6 06 26	6 06 26
Puritan . . .	12 25 45	2 17 00	5 32 43	6 38 39	6 12 54	6 11 40
Gracie . . .	12 27 00	2 29 47	6 00 36	7 12 34	6 45 34	6 35 59
Bedouin . .	12 27 00	2 41 40	6 00 25	7 26 10	6 59 10	6 49 32

The *Priscilla* defeated the *Puritan* 5 minutes 14 seconds ; the *Gracie*, 29 minutes 33 seconds ; the *Bedouin*, 43 minutes 6 seconds.

The *Priscilla* allowed the *Puritan* 1 minute 14 seconds ; the *Gracie*, 9 minutes 35 seconds ; the *Bedouin*, 9 minutes 38 seconds.

THE THIRD TRIAL RACE OCCURRED MONDAY, AUG. 24, 1885, and was over the regular inside course of the New York Yacht Club, starting from buoy 18, off Bay Ridge, to and around buoy 10, passing to the west and south of it; thence to buoy 8½, passing south of it, and north of buoy 5, off the point of Sandy Hook, to and around the Sandy Hook Lightship, leaving it on the starboard, and then returning over the same course, finishing at buoy 15. Distance, 38 miles.

There was a seven-knot breeze from the south-south-west, and the yachts crossed the starting-line in the following order: *Puritan*, 10 : 50 : 28 ; *Priscilla*, 10 : 50 : 30 ; *Gracie*, 10 : 50 : 46 ; and *Bedouin*, at 10 : 51 : 01 o'clock.

The interest in this race was, as before, centred in the two new sloops, and was still further heightened from the fact that the race would, without doubt, determine which of the two boats was to be selected to defend the Cup. A most exciting contest took place, resulting in another victory for the *Puritan*, under conditions of wind, etc., which were considered specially favorable to her foremost rival.

THE SUMMARY OF THE RACE.

COURSE. — 38 miles ; New York Yacht Club inside course.
WIND. — Average force about 7½ knots ; south-south-west.

	Start.	Buoy 8½.	Sandy Hook Lightship.	Buoy 10.	Finish.	Elapsed Time.	Corrected Time.
	H. M. S.	H. M. S.	H. M. S.	H. M. S.	H. M. S.	H. M. S.	H. M. S.
Puritan	10 50 28	12 02 45	12 51 50	2 04 28	2 43 05	3 52 37	3 51 26
Priscilla	10 50 30	12 04 10	12 53 01	2 06 10	2 43 48	3 53 18	3 53 18
Gracie	10 50 46	12 09 10	1 00 22	2 15 30	2 58 41	4 07 55	3 58 48
Bedouin	10 51 01	12 11 30	1 05 50	2 21 00	3 05 33	4 14 32	4 05 22

The *Puritan* defeated the *Priscilla* by 1 minute 52 seconds; the *Gracie*, by 7 minutes 22 seconds; the *Bedouin*, by 13 minutes 56 seconds.

The *Priscilla* allowed the *Puritan* 1 minute 11 seconds; the *Bedouin*, 9 minutes 10 seconds; the *Gracie*, 9 minutes 7 seconds.

The regatta committee subsequently discussed the relative merits of the *Puritan* and *Priscilla* under all conditions, and finally notified the owners of the *Puritan* that their boat had been selected to represent America in the coming international contest.

THE AMERICA'S CUP RACES OF 1885.

The date for the first race between the *Puritan* and the *Genesta*, for the possession of the America's Cup, was fixed for Monday, September 7. The interest in the races had been continually increasing, and at this time had reached a pitch wholly unparalleled in yachting history. The races and the respective merits of the rival boats became an absorbing topic of conversation among all classes of the community, and conjectures as to the result were heard on every hand.

The course fixed upon was that from the Scotland Lightship, off Sandy Hook, N.J., twenty miles to windward and return; and early on that bright September morning the grandest fleet ever seen in American waters, and probably in the world, moved down New York harbor to the starting-point. A light wind, north by west, prevailed. Scarcely a cloud could be seen, and the air was as balmy as in June. As 10.30 o'clock, the time for starting the race, approached, it was seen that the force of the wind was not sufficient to enable the yachts to go over the course in seven hours, — the time stipulated in the conditions of the race.

The wind subsequently shifted to the south-east and was blowing about five miles an hour, and increasing slightly. The committee decided to start the boats, and the preparatory signal was accordingly given at 1.31 o'clock. On board the *Puritan* were Messrs. Paine, Burgess, and Forbes, who took part with Capt. Crocker in the sailing of the yacht, while Sir Richard Sutton and Mr. Beavor-Webb assisted Capt. Carter on the *Genesta*. As the starting-whistle was blown, the *Puritan* was within one hundred feet of the line, over which she shot at 1:36:15, the *Genesta* following at 1:37:37 o'clock.

This contest, while it lasted, sufficed to show superior sailing qualities in the *Puritan* over those of the English cutter. Owing, however, to the failure of the wind, towards 6 o'clock, it became apparent to the committee that the yachts could not reach the finish line within the required seven hours from the start, and the race was of necessity declared off at 6.30 o'clock; the yachts at that time being near the outer mark-boat, and the *Puritan* holding a lead of fully two and one-half miles. The yachts were towed back and anchored in the Horseshoe, at Sandy Hook. Although there was much disappointment over the postponement, the results of the day's work gave great satisfaction to the champions of the *Puritan*. The centre-board sloop had shown her ability to outpoint and outfoot the cutter, for which such fine windward work had been claimed, and no fears as to her superiority in light winds were expressed.

THE SECOND ATTEMPT, SEPTEMBER 8. — On the following morning, Tuesday, September 8, the second attempt at a race was made, and ended in disappointment — even more keen than before. The breeze was fresh from the southeast, the weather being similar to that of the previous day, and there was every prospect of a splendid race. The two boats were in readiness for the contest and proceeded to the starting-point. The preparatory signal had been given, and the boats were waiting to receive the final signal, when, by some miscalculation on the part of the skippers on the *Puritan*, while attempting to cross the bows of the *Genesta*, in going to windward, the two boats were brought into too close proximity, and a collision ensued. The *Genesta's* bowsprit was driven through the *Puritan's* main-sail, making a large rent therein, and before it was possible to disengage it, the bowsprit was carried away and dragged helplessly over the *Genesta's* starboard bow.

The rent in the *Puritan's* main-sail was about a yard square, but she was otherwise uninjured. As the *Genesta's* bowsprit crashed over the side, tearing off stays and head-sails, the splendid discipline of her English crew was displayed to good advantage. There was no confusion; every man was in his place, and everything was speedily secured and stowed away. As the *Genesta* had the right of way, the committee immediately disqualified the *Puritan*. Sir Richard Sutton, however, refused to accede to the decision, and, with true sportsmanlike spirit, declared that he had come to America to test the relative merits of the cutter and centre-board sloop, and not to claim races on technicalities. The owners of the Boston sloop conferred with

Sir Richard, expressing profound regret for the accident, and offering to assume all the expense for repairs on the cutter. This offer, however, was refused by the *Genesta's* owner, who showed the most generous spirit throughout. Both yachts were immediately overhauled and put in thorough trim.

THE THIRD ATTEMPT, FRIDAY, SEPTEMBER 11. — Both yachts having been given a trial spin on the second day following the accident, to learn if everything was in proper condition, the next attempt was made on Friday, September 11, over the 20-mile windward course from Scotland Lightship. Indications pointed to a heavy sea and a good breeze; but the latter, although east-by-north and only about six knots, was increasing when the start was made.

The *Puritan* crossed the line at 11:35:41, and the *Genesta* at 11:35:48, the former being to windward. The *Puritan* had a decided advantage over the *Genesta* in this trial; but the hopes of those who had expected a race were agained doomed to disappointment, for the wind died down gradually, and at 4.30 o'clock the *Puritan*, which was leading by one and one-half miles, was still two miles distant from the mark-boat, and it became apparent that the race could not be finished. At 5.52 o'clock the judges set the signal for a postponement. The *Genesta* had not then rounded the mark, but the *Puritan* had rounded fifteen minutes before.

THE FOURTH ATTEMPT, SATURDAY, SEPTEMBER 12. — The fourth postponement occurred on Saturday, September 12, after the yachts had waited at the lightship until 2.25 o'clock, during which time there was almost a dead calm.

THE FIRST FINISHED RACE.

On Monday, Sept. 14, a race was sailed to the finish, and victory crowned the American sloop.

The course was the "inside" one of 38 miles, starting from buoy 18, off Bay Ridge, and was the same as that in the third trial race. The wind was light, from the south-west, at the time of starting, gradually falling away to almost a calm, and in the last half of the race freshening to ten miles an hour. When the starting signal was given, at 10.30 o'clock, the yachts were a considerable distance from the line, and, failing to cross within two minutes, time was computed from 10.32 o'clock. Both boats crossed a few seconds later, the *Genesta* being a short distance ahead, but slightly to leeward. The sloop was dressed in her main-sail, club-top-sail, forestay-sail, and jib, and the cutter carried the same sails, with jib-top-sail additional, though the latter was dispensed with soon after. The racers stood on the starboard tack for twelve minutes, during which the *Puritan* made a slight gain by pointing higher into the wind. On the next tack she gained about two hundred feet, and when they again tacked close by the Clifton shore another three hundred feet had been added, while she still held the weather position. Though losing momentarily by being blanketed by a large schooner on the next tack, she caught a six-knot breeze as she passed out of the Narrows, and at 11 o'clock was a good quarter of a mile to the fore. The *Genesta* had in the meantime set her jib-top-sail again. In the next half hour the white sloop had increased the lead to half a mile. About this time, however, she lost the breeze almost entirely, and the *Genesta*, holding it longer, closed a portion of the gap. The yachts sailed lazily, about a quarter of a mile apart, when the breeze returned, and the sloop first feeling its influence, regained a portion of the lost distance. Both boats then went under equal weather conditions, and the sloop showed the better speed, being at buoy 9 three-quarters of a mile in advance of her competitor, and an eighth of a mile to windward. At 12.30 o'clock the *Genesta* met baffling winds, and had much difficulty in weathering the buoy, and was losing steadily. The *Puritan* had opened a gap of nearly two miles, but during the next half-hour the cutter was more favored by the flukes and closed up considerably. Off the point of Sandy Hook there was the first indication of the *Genesta* overhauling the Boston boat, and there was great excitement. The latter was in a calm spot, and the cutter came bowling along at great speed.

The anxiety was soon relieved, however, for the *Puritan*, getting a fresh breeze before the *Genesta* had time to close up on her, shot away for the lightship at a rate which gave her a firm hold on her lead. The wind then blew ten miles an hour, and both boats carried all sail. It was a beautiful race to the lightship, the sloop outfooting the cutter steadily, and standing up better. The *Puritan* rounded the lightship at 2 : 14 : 54, and the *Genesta* at 2 : 19 : 16, — the former on the run home passing the latter half a mile to leeward of the ship. There was a great demonstration made by the fleet of excursion boats as each went off on the last half of the race. On the stretch back to buoy 10 the sloop did splendid sailing, and every inch of canvas did its work. She gained steadily in the fresh breeze, and when at the point of the Hook led by a mile. Inside the Hook both yachts had trouble with the strong ebb tide, and the wind there was found to be not over five miles an hour. Under these circumstances the cutter did better than the sloop; but the latter, on rounding buoy $8\frac{1}{2}$, at 3 : 32 : 30, set her balloon jib-top-sail, and from that moment to the finish she constantly crept ahead. The *Genesta* rounded buoy $8\frac{1}{2}$ at 3 : 38 : 05, and, with spinnaker and balloon jib-top-sail set, she started after her rival. She flew through the water, but failed to gain on the sloop, which did not set her spinnaker. The *Puritan* crossed the finish line at 4 : 38 : 05, and the *Genesta*, which was far astern, finished at 4 : 54 : 52. The joy of the thousands of spectators knew no bounds, and for many minutes whistles shrieked and cannons roared, proclaiming the great victory of the American centre-board sloop.

THE SUMMARY OF THE RACE.

COURSE. — 38 miles; New York Yacht Club inside course.
WIND. — Varying from one to ten miles an hour; southwest.

	Start.	Buoy No. 10.	Buoy No. 5.	Sandy Hook Lightship.	Buoy 10 (ret'g).	Finish.	Elapsed Time.	Corrected Time.
	H. M. S.	H. M. S.	H. M. S.	H. M. S.	H. M. S.	H. M. S.	H. M. S.	H. M. S.
Puritan.	10 32 00	1 16 32	1 31 30	2 14 54	3 38 05	4 38 05	6 06 05	6 06 05
Genesta.	10 32 00	1 19 25	1 36 00	2 19 16	3 46 05	4 54 52	6 22 52	6 22 24

The *Puritan* allowed the *Genesta* 28 seconds, and won by 16 minutes 19 seconds, corrected time.

THE SECOND FINISHED RACE.

On Wednesday, September 16, the second race to a finish was sailed; and, though the Boston sloop won, it was only after a battle the outcome of which was uncertain almost to the moment the *Puritan* crossed the finish line. The course was that from the lightship *Wreck of Scotland*, twenty miles dead to leeward and return. The wind was west-north-west, blowing ten miles an hour; and, with spinnaker, main-sail, and club-top-sail set, the *Genesta* started at 11:05:16, and the *Puritan* at 11:06:01. Both went like greyhounds, but the white sloop, inch by inch, closed up, and at 11.50 o'clock was abreast of the cutter. About this time the *Genesta* changed her spinnaker from starboard to port, and the change helped her perceptibly. During the next five miles she slowly gained on the centre-board, which had gone to the front during the shifting of canvas, and at 12.45 o'clock passed to the fore. The visitor continued to excel in speed, and after a magnificent run reached the mark-boat a half-mile in the lead. She rounded at 1:05:30, and the *Puritan* made the turn 2 minutes and 6 seconds later. Both started on the beat homeward on the starboard tack, and here the sloop did some phenomenal work. The wind had increased to nearly twenty miles an hour, and both continued the fight with whole main-sails, club-top-sails, and two jibs. The *Puritan* slowly worked to windward, and when both tacked to port, at 1.22, the *Genesta's* lead had been decreased to a quarter of a mile. The *Puritan* sent down her topmast at 1.26 o'clock, and the *Genesta* took in her top-sail at the same time. The weather was now squally, and as it increased in force the *Puritan* continued to outpoint and outfoot the cutter. At 2 o'clock both yachts were sailing with their lee rails under water and their decks awash, the wind blowing at the rate of nearly thirty miles an hour; but in fifteen minutes the wind had subsided to twenty knots. In going about on the starboard tack, at 2.16 o'clock, the *Puritan* showed that she had recovered her loss, and was a mile to windward. Another increase in the wind sent it up to thirty knots an hour, and caused an ugly sea, in which the *Genesta* labored heavily. The *Puritan*, however, lost some of her gain to windward by the wind hauling to the north-north-west. The *Genesta*, though previously far to leeward, could now make the lightship in one long reach of ten miles, and the result of the race became a matter of grave doubt. The *Puritan* overcame this advantage by heading up a trifle higher, while still maintaining a pace equal to that of the cutter, and for a time the boats, bow and bow, rushed madly through the water. It was a most exciting struggle; and the anxiety, as the yachts approached the finish line, was intense. At two miles from the lightship the *Puritan* was a trifle to windward and leading by only a few feet. Capt. Carter made a desperate attempt to take his vessel into the weather position, but in vain. He again and again repeated the attempt; but at one mile from the line the white boat had secured a safe lead, and a few minutes later had crossed, a winner of the race and of the America's Cup. The demonstration in honor of the victory was one long to be remembered. Human voices, cannons, and whistles sounded their applause, and excursionists danced with delight, embraced each other, and gave all sorts of evidence of joy. The salute to the *Genesta* when she finished was hardly less demonstrative.

THE SUMMARY OF THE RACE.

COURSE. — 20 miles to leeward and return, starting from Scotland Lightship.

WIND. — Varying from ten to thirty miles an hour; west-north-west at the start, and shifting to north-north-west during the last half of the race.

	Start.	Turning Stake.	Finish.	Elapsed Time.	Corrected Time.
	H. M. S.	H. M. S.	H. M. S.	H. M. S.	H. M. S.
Puritan .	11 06 01	1 07 36	4 09 15	5 03 14	5 03 14
Genesta .	11 05 16	1 05 30	4 10 39	5 05 23	5 04 52

The *Puritan* allowed the *Genesta* 31 seconds, and won by 1 minute 38 seconds, corrected time.

Soon after the cup races the *Puritan* was sold at auction to Gen. Charles J. Paine, of Boston, and was purchased from him, before the opening of the next yachting season, by Mr. J. Malcolm Forbes, Vice-Commodore of the Eastern Yacht Club, and is now in his possession.

THE CHALLENGE OF THE *GALATEA*.

The challenge from Mr. J. Beavor-Webb was received February 26, 1885, he having entered the English cutter *Galatea*, as well as the *Genesta*, for the race for the

America's Cup. That part of the manifesto which related to the *Galatea* was accepted at a meeting of the New York Yacht Club, on October 22, 1885, and the races were fixed for the following year. No modifications in the sailing regulations were made, although several were suggested by the owner of the challenging boat.

THE BOSTON CENTRE-BOARD SLOOP *MAYFLOWER*.

To the liberality and public spirit of Gen. Charles J. Paine, of Boston, unaided by any syndicate, as in the case of the building of the sloop *Puritan*, is due the sloop *Mayflower*, which achieved great honors over America's fastest yachts of all classes, as well as securing the renown of successfully defending the challenge for the America's Cup in 1886. The entire cost was assumed by him, and to rigging and sailing her his best efforts were given during the memorable yachting season of that year.

The *Mayflower* was designed by Mr. Edward Burgess, of Boston, many of General Paine's ideas being embodied in the plans.

Mr. Burgess frankly said at the time: "It is only fair to General Paine to state that the principal changes made in the new sloop, which cause her to differ from the *Puritan*, were made under his direction. They are the outcome of his ideas, and, if she comes up to what is expected, General Paine should have all the credit."

The plans were delivered early in the year 1886 to Messrs. George Lawley & Sons, of South Boston, who began the work of construction on January 25. She was built entirely of wood, of the best material, and the

work of construction was the most thorough in every respect. On the 6th day of May the *Mayflower* was successfully launched, and the work of rigging her speedily followed. The general appearance of the *Mayflower* is not unlike that of the *Puritan*. In many particulars, however, there is a wide difference between them. The frames, forty-nine in number, are all double, except the seven forward and three after cants, and are of oak, as are also the chain-plate frames, which extend in one piece from keel to gunwale. All the frames are mortised into the side of the keel, and those in the wake of the centre-board are dovetailed and keyed. The keel is made of two oak logs, each being originally sixty feet long and twenty-three inches square. The stern-post is attached to the keel by a knee, to which it is bolted. The centre-board well is cut in the keel, twenty-three feet long and five inches wide. The oak keel is about sixty-eight feet long, and is in its widest part, along the centre-board slot, forty-six inches on top and forty inches on the bottom. The lead keel originally weighed thirty-seven tons, but this weight was increased subsequently. It was run in three moulds, to conform to the oak keel, the forward piece being about fourteen feet long, the middle one about twenty-three feet long, and the after piece about twenty feet long. Along the centre-board box this enormous mass of lead measures forty inches wide at the top, and sixteen inches at the lowest part. It is attached to the oak keel by heavy bolts of yellow metal. The stem and the stern-post are of the best white oak. The latter has a rake of four feet and three inches in nine feet and eight inches.

The centre-board is twenty-two feet long, ten feet deep,

and four inches thick. Its lower courses are of oak, and its upper ones of hard pine. Several hundred pounds of lead in the top serve to sink it easily. There are twelve iron floor timbers, — six forward and six aft of the centre-board box, which weigh about two tons, and serve as ballast as well as to strengthen the vessel. The deck beams are of hackmatack, 6 × 5 inches. The deck is laid in the best white pine. The bulwarks are also of white pine, the rail of oak, and the stringers of yellow pine. The chain-plates are of iron, six in number, three on each side of the vessel.

The main saloon is fifteen feet long, and of nearly the same beam as the yacht, the trimmings being of mahogany. There is an after state-room, seven feet long, with two berths; on the starboard side, forward of the main saloon, a large state-room, with modern conveniences, and on the port side, forward, several small state-rooms for the officers. The galley and forecastle are conveniently furnished and well lighted and ventilated.

The sailing master selected for the *Mayflower* was Capt. Martin V. B. Stone, of Swampscott, Mass., who since his boyhood had had experience in sailing craft and had gained an excellent reputation as a sailing master of racing yachts, by his splendid handling of the speedy schooner yacht *Halcyon*, while she was owned by General Paine.

The trial trip of the *Mayflower* was made on May 30, 1886, but did not afford an opportunity to show the real merits of the yacht, owing to the fact that the new sails sat very badly. Frequent trips in Massachusetts Bay caused an improvement in the sails; but in several regattas she was defeated by the *Puritan*, although she showed wonderful speed in running and reaching. Slight changes in spars, sails, and ballast were at once made, and resulted in some improvement in the sailing qualities of the yacht, for in the next contest in which she was entered — the annual cruise of the New York Yacht Club — she led the fleet of seventy vessels, the run being from New London, Conn., to Newport, R.I.

In the race for the Goelet Cup for sloops, on Aug. 7, 1886, the *Mayflower* was the victor, and over the whole course of forty-four miles she gave a wonderful performance, defeating the fleet-footed *Puritan*, *Atlantic*, and *Priscilla*.

General Paine, from the beginning of the season, had labored incessantly to remedy the defects natural to a new yacht, and to Mr. Burgess's skill in designing was added the valuable suggestions as to sails and ballasting which the owner of the craft had learned by long experience in yachting contests. To defend the challenge for the America's Cup, which had been sent by Mr. J. Beavor-Webb in behalf of Lieut. William R. Henn, the owner of the British cutter *Galatea*, was General Paine's sole object for the enormous outlay of money in building the *Mayflower*, and to his untiring energy was due the credit of bringing to the front the fleetest yacht that had ever been produced on American shores. After the changes in the *Mayflower*, which have been noted, had been made, the official measurements were as follows: —

Length over all, 100 feet; length on water-line, 85 feet 7 inches; beam, 23 feet $6\frac{1}{2}$ inches; beam at water-line, 22 feet 3 inches; depth of hold, 8 feet 6 inches; draught,

10 feet; length of mast from deck to hounds, 63 feet; length of top-mast, entire, 48 feet; length of boom, 80 feet; length of gaff, 50 feet; length of bowsprit, outboard, 38 feet; length of spinnaker-boom, 67 feet; displacement, 128 tons; ballast, inside and keel, 50 tons; sail area (New York Yacht Club rules), 8,634 square feet; racing measurement (New York Yacht Club rules), 87.99.

In this condition the *Mayflower* prepared to do battle with the *Galatea*.

THE ENGLISH CUTTER *GALATEA*.

The English cutter *Galatea*, which was the challenging boat entered for the America's Cup races in 1886, was designed by Mr. J. Beavor-Webb and owned by Lieut. William R. Henn, R.N.

The *Galatea* was launched on May 1, 1885, having been built by Messrs. John Reid & Sons, of Port Glasgow, Scot. The hull is wholly of steel, and the deck, fittings, bulwarks, and stanchions are of teak. Her keel is of steel, trough-shaped, into which eighty tons of lead were run, this being the total amount of ballast. The workmanship was of the finest order possible. Beneath her coat of paint, which is as smooth as glass, neither rivet nor butt is seen. Her inside fittings are excellent. The main saloon is panelled in walnut and ash, and was designed with much taste. The after-cabin is finished in Hungarian ash, and the cabinet work is of beautiful design. Much difficulty was experienced in getting her in perfect trim, and in the races in which she took part in her first season she was particularly unfortunate. In

GALATEA.

three races she met with serious accidents, one of which was the carrying away of her mast close to the deck. She was entered in fifteen races during the season of 1885, but did not secure a first prize. Three second prizes were her only trophies, as in most of the events she was badly defeated by the crack English yachts *Irex*, *Marjorie*, *Wendur*, and *Marguerite*. At the end of the season the *Galatea* was thoroughly overhauled and her ballast recast lower than before. Her record in 1886 continued to be poor, for in the three races which she sailed in British waters she won but two second prizes. Many experiments were made with her main-sail, and a loose-footed one was finally deemed to be the best suited to her. Commanded by Capt. Daniel Bradford, an experienced English navigator, the *Galatea* sailed for America on the 30th day of June, 1886, and dropped anchor in the harbor of Marblehead, Mass., on the evening of August 1, after an uneventful voyage. Subsequently she sailed for New York, where she was placed in a dry dock, to be overhauled and made ready for the Cup races.

By the rules of the New York Yacht Club the official measurements of the *Galatea* were found to be as follows: —

Length over all, 102.60 feet; length on water-line, 86.80 feet; beam, 15 feet; draught, 13.50 feet; area of midship section, 110 feet; length of mast, deck to hounds, 53 feet; length of top-mast, 51 feet; length of boom, 73 feet; length of gaff, 46 feet; length of bowsprit, outboard, 37.60 feet; length of spinnaker-boom, 67 feet; ballast, 80 tons; displacement, 157.63 tons; sail area (New York

Yacht Club rules), 7,505 square feet; racing measurement (New York Yacht Club rules), 86.87.

THE TRIAL RACES OF 1886.

The first trial race took place on Saturday, Aug. 21, 1886, over the New York Yacht Club inside course; distance, 38 miles. The entries were: —
Puritan, centre-board sloop, Boston, racing measurement, 83.85; *Mayflower*, centre-board sloop, Boston, racing measurement, 87.99; *Atlantic*, centre-board sloop, New York, racing measurement, 86.31; *Priscilla*, centre-board sloop, New York, racing measurement, 85.97.

The *Atlantic* had been built during the previous winter for a syndicate of New York gentlemen, for the express purpose of defending the challenge for the Cup. She is a centre-board sloop, constructed of wood, and was designed by Mr. Philip Elsworth. Mr. John F. Mumm, of Brooklyn, N. Y., was her builder, and she was launched on May 1, 1886.

During the past year slight changes had been made in the rig of the *Priscilla*, and she had passed into the hands of Mr. A. Cass Canfield.

The wind was light from the east-south-east, and when the boats crossed the line the *Atlantic* held the weather position, with the *Puritan* on her lee-quarter and the *Priscilla* a trifle farther to leeward. The *Mayflower* was some distance astern, but when she crossed was well up to windward. The time of the start was: *Atlantic*, 10:12:07; *Puritan*, 10:12:50; *Priscilla*, 10:13:20; *Mayflower*, 10:14:26. The *Mayflower*, 2 minutes 19 seconds in the rear of the *Atlantic*, began to force the battle at the start. Pointed high in the wind, she went along at a pace which the *Puritan* could not hold so close to the wind. She gradually closed up on the latter, and in the run to the light-ship passed the two New-Yorkers. The lightship was rounded by the *Mayflower* at 1:36:40; by the *Atlantic* at 1:44:40; by the *Puritan* at 1:46:05; and by the *Priscilla* at 1:50:10; and they all started homeward with their spinnakers out. The *Mayflower* continued to widen the gap, and at the finish line led the *Atlantic*, her nearest competitor, by over a mile.

THE SUMMARY OF THE FIRST RACE.

COURSE. — 38 miles; New York Yacht Club inside course.
WIND. — Light; east-south-east.

	Start.	Sandy Hook Lightship.	Finish.	Elapsed Time.	Corrected Time.
	H. M. S.	H. M. S.	H. M. S.	H. M. S.	H. M. S.
Mayflower . .	10 14 26	1 36 40	3 51 10	5 36 44	5 36 44
Atlantic . . .	10 12 07	1 44 40	4 00 42	5 48 35	5 47 34
Puritan . . .	10 12 50	1 46 05	4 03 11	5 50 21	5 47 55
Priscilla . . .	10 13 20	1 50 10	4 09 45	5 56 25	5 55 13

The *Mayflower* won by 10 minutes 50 seconds, corrected time.

The *Mayflower* allowed the *Atlantic* 1 minute 1 second; the *Priscilla*, 1 minute 12 seconds; the *Puritan*, 2 minutes 26 seconds.

On Monday, August 23, an attempt was made to sail the second trial-race, but after the yachts had sailed ten miles the wind gave out, and a postponement resulted. The

Puritan was then in the lead, the *Mayflower* second, the *Priscilla* third, and the *Atlantic*, which had carried away her top-mast, was out of the race.

The second trial race occurred on Wednesday, August 25, over a course fifteen miles to leeward and return. The wind was north-north-east, and the run was south-south-west, the start being from Sandy Hook Lightship, three miles farther out than the Scotland Lightship. With a steady 20-knot breeze, the race proved to be a grand one. The *Mayflower* started with a handicap of 2 minutes 25 seconds, but nearly overhauled her rivals before the outer mark was reached. The beat homeward showed that the *Mayflower* was the superior of the other flyers in strong winds as much as she had been in light winds, and at the finish she led the *Puritan* by half a mile, and the others by over a mile.

THE SUMMARY OF THE SECOND RACE.

COURSE. — 30 miles; 15 miles to leeward and return, starting from Sandy Hook Lightship.

WIND. — 20 miles an hour; north-north-east.

	Start.	Outer Mark.	Finish.	Elapsed Time.	Corrected Time.
	H. M. S.	H. M. S.	H. M. S.	H. M. S.	H. M. S.
Mayflower . .	12 09 00	2 21 31	4 50 45	4 41 49	4 41 49
Puritan . . .	12 07 36	2 22 30	4 55 05	4 47 29	4 45 36
Priscilla . . .	12 09 00	2 23 17	4 59 47	4 50 47	4 49 50
Atlantic . . .	12 06 38	2 20 02	4 58 58	4 52 20	4 51 32

The *Mayflower* won by 3 minutes 47 seconds, corrected time. The *Mayflower* allowed the *Atlantic* 48 seconds;

RACE BETWEEN MAYFLOWER AND GALATEA.
INSIDE COURSE, SEPTEMBER 7, 1886.

the *Priscilla*, 57 seconds; the *Puritan*, 1 minute 53 seconds.

The committee immediately selected the *Mayflower* as the defender of the challenge for the America's Cup.

THE CUP RACES OF 1886.

THE FIRST RACE, TUESDAY, SEPT. 7. — The course chosen for the first race was the regular one of the New York Yacht Club, starting from buoy 18, New York harbor, and the same as the one sailed over by the *Puritan* and *Genesta* in the "inside" race of the previous year. Interest in yachting in general, and in this event in particular, had been intensified by the races of 1885, and throughout the country news of the progress of the struggle was eagerly sought. In Boston the enthusiasm of the previous season was unabated. At the scene of the contest there was the same dazzling picture as before. Speedy and costly steam yachts mingled with lowly craft of all descriptions. Sailing yachts, with huge spread of canvas, darted hither and thither to avoid the immense flotilla of tugs, steamers, and steam yachts, and the shores on both sides were black with people, who all day long gazed upon the grand marine spectacle.

The wind was from the south, compelling the yachts to beat down the Narrows, and was very light. As the prospect that it would increase in force was good, the committee having charge of the race decided to start the boats, and the preparatory signal was given. Then there began the most skilful sailing for position of which yachtsmen are capable, and sharp tactics were resorted to.

The *Galatea*, however, held the most advantageous position, and was able to keep it until the signal for the start was given, when she shot over the line at 10:56:11; the *Mayflower* following at 10:56:12 o'clock. Both yachts crossed on the starboard tack, the *Mayflower* carrying her main-sail, club-top-sail, forestay-sail, jib and jib-top-sail, and the *Galatea* the same, except that her jib-top-sail was not set. The start was a magnificent one, and was accompanied by a deafening roar of cannon and shriek of whistles from the attendant fleet. The *Galatea* being to windward, the *Mayflower* made an effort to prevent being blanketed, and soon crept a few feet to the front. The visitor, however, was pointing closer into the wind. As they neared the Bay Ridge shore, the sloop had a lead of two hundred feet, and, going about on the port tack, was nearly on even terms. The *Galatea* tacked immediately, and showed herself to be much quicker in stays. In standing toward the Staten Island shore, the cutter was jammed so closely into the wind that she moved heavily through the water, and the *Mayflower* was making a very perceptible gap between herself and her rival. Both were affected by the strong flood-tide which was setting them to leeward, the *Galatea* suffering more than the *Mayflower*. At 11:03:30 the cutter's jib-top-sail was run up, but it did not prevent the *Mayflower* from still drawing away from her. As the yachts approached the Stapleton shore they found a large schooner anchored in their path. The *Mayflower* tried to weather it, and by luffing succeeded, but the English boat was obliged to go to leeward of it. Both kept close to the shore, the sloop going about at 11:13:30, and the cutter at 11:14:30 o'clock.

On this stretch the *Mayflower* made a considerable gain. She did not attempt to sail so high into the wind, but under skilful handling kept good headway, and in the light wind did creditable work. Mr. Beavor-Webb held the tiller of the iron boat, and Captain Stone was at the *Mayflower's* wheel, while the assistance and suggestions of Messrs. Paine and Burgess were invaluable. The *Galatea* was being pinched hard to offset in windward work what the *Mayflower* was doing in outfooting her, and was fully a quarter of a mile astern when the latter tacked, at 11 : 22 : 20. Short tacks ensued, the *Mayflower* making fifteen and the *Galatea* sixteen from the start to buoy 10, the sloop then leading fully three-fourths of a mile. The *Mayflower* rounded buoy $8\frac{1}{2}$ at 1 : 01 : 51, and the *Galatea* at 1 : 07 : 07. From this point to the end of Sandy Hook the *Galatea* decreased the gap by holding better to windward against the tide than did the American boat. It was one long reach to the Sandy Hook Lightship, and the *Mayflower's* splendid sailing qualities added three minutes more to her advantage. She rounded the lightship on the starboard tack at 2 : 35 : 02, and her immense balloon jib-topsail was immediately broken out. The *Galatea* rounded at 2 : 44 : 13, and likewise set her balloon jib-top-sail, though by no means with the skill displayed by the Yankee crew. In the reach back to the Hook, the sloop gained three minutes more, and passed buoy $8\frac{1}{2}$ at 3.34, followed by the *Galatea* at 3.46 o'clock. With a slightly freshening wind, the boats began their run home before it, though the Boston boat did not set her spinnaker until she was within a mile of the finish. Five minutes before the cutter's spinnaker had been set, and both boats were bowling along at good speed, accompanied by the fleet of steam craft which crowded in on all sides. The *Mayflower* finished at 5 : 26 : 41, with a lead of one and one-half miles, and the *Galatea* at 5 : 39 : 21. Each received a salute, which continued for many minutes, steam-whistles and cannons sounding their loud acclaim.

THE SUMMARY OF THE RACE.

COURSE. — 38 miles; New York Yacht Club inside course.
WIND. — Light; south.

	Start.	Buoy S¼.	Sandy Hook Lightship.	Buoy S½ (ret'g).	Finish.	Elapsed Time.	Corrected Time.
	H. M. S.	H. M. S.	H. M. S.	H. M. S.	H. M. S.	H. M. S.	H. M. S.
Mayflower	10 56 12	1 01 51	2 35 02	3 34 00	4 22 53	5 26 41	5 26 41
Galatea	10 56 11	1 07 07	2 44 13	3 46 00	4 35 32	5 39 21	5 38 43

The *Mayflower* won by 12 minutes 2 seconds, corrected time.
The *Mayflower* allowed the *Galatea* 38 seconds.

THE SECOND DAY, THURSDAY, SEPT. 9. — A POSTPONE-
MENT. — On Thursday, September 9, the day fixed for the second race, the weather was anything but favorable. There was a light rain, a fog, at times thick, and a moderate breeze east by north. The course was to be twenty miles to windward from the Scotland Lightship and return to the starting-point, and the yachts, anticipating bad weather, carried none of their flying kites. The *Galatea* had reefed her bowsprit and carried a No. 2 jib, working-top-sail,

forestay-sail, and main-sail. The start was made with the boats on the starboard tack, the *Mayflower* being a trifle to windward. The latter crossed at 11 : 30 : 30, and the *Galatea* at 11 : 30 : 32. The sloop slowly drew ahead, the wind meanwhile becoming lighter and lighter. Club-top-sails were set in place of working ones. The run out was uninteresting, it being almost certain that the race would not be finished. The fog had become so thick that it was impossible to judge of the relative positions of the boats, and the committee's boat, *Luckenbach*, had difficulty in finding the mark-boat. At 4 : 26 : 22 the *Mayflower* rounded the mark, and, with spinnaker set to port, began her homeward run. The *Galatea* failed to find the mark-boat, and turned her prow homeward, but did not thereby lose the race, as the *Mayflower* failed to reach the lightship within the time-limit. It was a day which could hardly be exceeded in discomfort and disappointment.

THE SECOND RACE, SATURDAY, SEPT. 11. — The Cup races for 1886 came to an end on Saturday, September 11, when the *Mayflower* showed her heels to the English cutter, and won the race and the Cup. The run was twenty miles to leeward and return, starting from Scotland Lightship, and the wind at the start was from the north-west at the rate of twelve miles an hour. With spinnaker to port the *Mayflower* flew over the starting-line at 11 : 22 : 40, and immediately broke out her balloon jib-top-sail, the *Galatea* crossing at 11 : 24 : 10, and setting her spinnaker just after she crossed. The skill with which the sloop was handled had given her an advantage at the start. She was under the influence of her big canvas in going over the line, and started off at great speed. The *Galatea* followed directly in her wake, but, being over a minute behind, failed to take the wind out of the *Mayflower's* sails. In fact, the Boston sloop was constantly making the distance between them greater and greater. It was a steady gain, and as mile after mile was covered the lead showed the remarkable powers of the sloop. The *Galatea's* balloon jib-top-sail had not been set, but it was claimed that sailing before the wind was the strong point of the English boat. However, the sloop outfooted her all the time, and when the latter took in her spinnaker, a mile from the mark-boat, the cutter was a mile and a half astern. The *Mayflower* jibed before reaching the mark, and rounded, at 1:55:05, on the starboard tack. At the same time the *Galatea's* spinnaker was taken in, and it was not until 2:10:20 that she rounded, the *Mayflower* in the meantime making a great increase in her lead. The cutter rounded on the starboard tack, and began her windward work with main-sail, club-top-sail, forestay-sail, jib, and jib-top-sail, and the *Mayflower* carried the same, excepting the jib-top-sail. Both stood off on this tack for a long time, during which the *Mayflower* kept working up to windward more than her rival, although the latter was then giving the best display of her abilities that had thus far been seen. At 4 o'clock the *Mayflower* had made but two tacks since leaving the mark-boat, and the *Galatea* had not gone about at all since rounding. Both were standing in close to the New Jersey shore in the hope of getting more wind. For an hour the breeze had been dying out, and the sloop was the greater loser. The *Galatea* then began to reduce the *Mayflower's* lead, which at one time had been over two miles; but soon after 4 o'clock the racers became almost becalmed. A light breeze soon after sprang up, and the sloop was the first to get the advantage of it. The American boat was well up to windward and closer in shore, and here she ran away from the cutter, which could not get the benefit of the light off-shore breeze. At 5.30 o'clock, with the *Mayflower* about four miles from the finish, and the *Galatea* nearly the same distance astern of her, the wind again decreased. The yachts moved lazily along, and for a time it was doubtful if the race could be finished within the time-limit. It was a most unsatisfactory exhibition of yacht-racing; but the *Mayflower* finally reached the goal, with but eleven minutes of the seven hours to spare. Former demonstrations in honor of the Boston sloop were repeated by the thousands of excursionists, and the *Mayflower* was proclaimed the winner of the America's Cup.

THE SUMMARY OF THE RACE.

COURSE. — 20 miles to leeward and return, starting from Scotland Lightship.

WIND. — 12 miles an hour at the start, averaging about 4 miles an hour during last half of the race; northwest.

	Start.	Outer Mark.	Finish.	Elapsed Time.	Corrected Time.
	H. M. S.	H. M. S.	H. M. S.	H. M. S.	H. M. S.
Mayflower .	11 22 40	1 55 05	6 11 40	6 49 00	6 49 00
Galatea . . .	11 24 10	2 10 20	6 42 58	7 18 48	7 18 09

The *Mayflower* won by 29 minutes 9 seconds, corrected time. The *Mayflower* allowed the *Galatea* 39 seconds.

In July, 1887, General Paine disposed of the *Mayflower* to Mr. E. D. Morgan, of the New York Yacht Club, her present owner.

THE *THISTLE'S* CHALLENGE IN 1887.

In the fall of the year 1886 the New York Yacht Club was notified by the Royal Clyde Yacht Club of an intention to challenge for the America's Cup, and the cutter *Thistle* was named as the Scottish representative. The formal challenge was received from Mr. William York, secretary of the Royal Clyde Club, on March 28, 1887, and was accepted on the following day. In addition to several suggestions of minor importance, Mr. York asked that there be five instead of three races, and that they be sailed in October. This request, however, the Cup committee decided not to grant, and the races were arranged for September, under the same regulations as in the previous year.

THE STEEL CENTRE-BOARD SLOOP *VOLUNTEER*.

During the fall of 1886 Mr. George L. Watson, the leading yacht designer of Great Britain, had visited America, and, by a careful inspection of our fleetest boats, had obtained many valuable ideas in regard to yacht-designing and building, and on his return to Scotland had begun work on the plans of the cutter *Thistle*, the challenger for the America's Cup in 1887. It was then reported that his forthcoming yacht would be of phenomenal speed, combining the best points of American as well as English racers. But General Paine and Mr. Burgess were

not content to rest upon their past achievements, and were determined to show that America could also improve in yacht-designing. Again did General Paine assert his patriotic spirit, and again did Mr. Burgess display his skill. When the measurements of the *Thistle* became known, in the spring of 1887, Mr. Burgess immediately began work on the designs of a steel centre-board sloop of about the same water-line length as the *Thistle*, and General Paine immediately stepped to the front in defence of the Cup, and bore the entire expense of building and fitting out a yacht from the new designs. The result was the *Volunteer*, the fastest sloop in the world. The builders were Messrs. Pusey & Jones, of Wilmington, Del. The *Thistle* was then nearly ready to be launched and put in proper trim, and it was necessary that speedy work should be done to build the *Volunteer* in time to give her a thorough trial before her contest for the America's Cup. In consequence of the limited time, the plating of the steel hull was not as smooth as it would otherwise have been.

The *Volunteer's* ballast is stowed two feet lower than the oak keels will allow in the *Puritan* and *Mayflower*, and this gives her greater stability than the two latter boats possess. The frames are of steel, spaced twenty-one inches on centres, and along the centre-board well there are twenty-two angle-iron frames. The well is plated with steel. The outside plating is steel, and is flushed from keel to gunwale. The keel-plating, three-fourths of an inch in thickness, is riveted to transverse frames. In the trough in which the ballast is stowed there is a steel floorplate at each frame, and in these spaces molten lead was run, thus making solid ballast. The deck-beams are made of angle iron, $3 \times 4 \times \frac{6}{16}$ inches thick. To counteract the strain of the mast, the frames along the sides, opposite the mast, are strengthened by steel brackets riveted to the frames and deck beams. At the turn of the bilge, and between the cabin floor and keel, the hull is stiffened by two thick steel strakes. The planksheer is of white pine. The waist has locust stanchions and the rail is of oak. Her deck is flush and of white pine. Her bow, unlike the Cup defenders of 1885 and 1886, is an overhanging one, but the stern differs very slightly. Compared with the *Mayflower* she has less beam and more bilge. Her greatest vantage point over the *Mayflower*, however, is in her lower centre of gravity. Her chain-plates run along the frames on the inside of the plating, thus leaving her sides clean. The bowsprit is a reefing one, the first to be put on a Burgess sloop of the first class, and it can be shortened eight feet. Steel wire is used for the main rigging, and above, as well as below, decks, the strongest and best materials were employed in her construction. On each side of the centre-board box there is a passage, and leading out of each there are two state-rooms, which are conveniently fitted up and neatly furnished. The main saloon contains two berths on each side, and aft there is a good-sized state-room. The quarters of the crew are roomy, light, and well ventilated. There is ample room, and, while it was sought to attain speed, it should not be inferred that the *Volunteer* is a mere racing-machine. Minor changes only were made in her during the season, and her measurements at the time of the Cup races were as follows: —

Length over all, 106.23 feet; length on water-line, 85.88 feet; beam, 23 feet 2 inches; draught, 10 feet; length of mast, from deck to hounds, 63 feet; length of topmast, 48 feet; length of boom, 84 feet; length of gaff, 51 feet 6 inches; length of bowsprit, outboard, 38 feet; length of spinnaker-boom, 67 feet; displacement, 130 tons; ballast, inside and keel, 55 tons; sail area (New York Yacht Club rules), 9,260 square feet; racing measurement (New York Yacht Club rules), 89.35.

Capt. Henry Haff, of Islip, L.I., was selected as sailing master of the new boat during the season of 1887. He had many times sailed the sloop *Fanny*, of New York, to victory, and was, through long experience in yacht sailing, in every way competent to handle the new Burgess boat. The maiden trip of the *Volunteer*, under sail, was made on July 21, 1887, and she gave great satisfaction. She subsequently proved to be a marvellous boat. Mr. Burgess had not only exceeded his previous efforts, but he had produced a boat which, under the skilful guidance of General Paine, was the wonder of the yachting world. Her record was phenomenal, and during the whole season was one long list of victories for Boston skill and enterprise. Though racing with new and unstretched sails, she readily ran away from the fleet-footed *Mayflower*, *Puritan*, *Atlantic*, and *Priscilla*, capturing the Goelet Cup, in a race off Newport, on August 5; the Morgan Cup, in a run from Vineyard Haven to Marblehead, on August 8 and 9; the "Boston Herald" Cup,[1]

---

[1] The "Herald" Cup is undoubtedly the most elaborate, and also the most costly, trophy that has ever been contended for in yachting circles in our waters. It is of solid silver, .925 fine, and is said to be the largest piece of silver work ever made in Boston. It is in the form of a large bowl resting upon four conch-shells, beautifully modelled. Its weight is 310 ounces; it measures 16 inches across the top, and has a capacity of

in a race off Marblehead, on August 11; and the Providence and Newport Citizens' Cups, on August 15 and 16. The value of these trophies was about $4,000.

THE SCOTCH CUTTER *THISTLE*.

The Scotch cutter *Thistle* was designed for the express purpose of competing for the America's Cup. The failures of the *Genesta* and *Galatea* to capture the coveted trophy had aroused the enthusiasm of the Scotchmen, and in September, 1886, a party of Clyde yachtsmen determined to issue a challenge and send to America a boat of Scottish design and build and manned by a Scottish crew. The money for building the new boat was subscribed by Messrs. John Clark, Commodore of the Royal Clyde Yacht Club, William Clark, Andrew Coates, William Coates, James Coates, George Coates, J. Hilliard, James Bell, Vice-Commodore of the Royal Clyde Yacht Club, and William Bell.

The designer was Mr. George L. Watson, the most skilful naval architect in the British Isles. Aided by the knowledge gained from a careful study of our yachts and

---

5 gallons. The shells which form the feet were modelled from the finest varieties of a conchologist, castings being made and exact fac-simile of each produced. The three sides, or panels, of the cup are alike in design, except that the shields bear different legends. Every raised line and indentation seems typical of the sea. Mermaids or water-nymphs rise out of the crest of the swelling ocean and hold aloft garlands of marine plants with which to crown the victor, and also display conch-shells, typical of success. Down deeper in the trough of the sea is old Neptune, struggling bravely upward, with an ancient form of paddle in his right hand, while with his left he holds aloft a shield bearing the record of victory, and under his arm is a sea-horse, from which outpours a rush of water which flows through the kelp and weeds and pads which everywhere abound. The handles and sockets are made to represent aquatic plants, and even the rim of the cup, in its undulating form, suggests the wave-motion of the sea.

the waters in which the Cup races in America are sailed, he delivered to the syndicate the plans of a cutter which was destined to eclipse the performances of all of England's most famous racers. The new boat, which was subsequently named the *Thistle*, was built by Messrs. D. & W. Henderson, at Partick. The utmost secrecy in regard to her was preserved from the outset. The yard in which she was built was kept securely locked, and every effort was made to keep her water-line length a secret. Even when she was launched, on April 26, 1887, she was covered with canvas, to hide her lines from the eyes of the public. The *Thistle* is a steel cutter, and differs from the modern English cutter in having her forefoot more cut away and in her greater beam. Her sides are much rounder, and flare up from the load water-line to the planksheer. Her hull is plated with the best Siemens-Martin steel, the lower plates being three-quarters, and the upper five-sixteenths, of an inch thick. The three lower strakes have lap seams, but the top body is plated flush. The frames are of unusual strength, and are tied by steel diagonals, stringers, keelsons, and floorings, forming a network of the most secure description. Partial bulkheads give still further strength, and there is also, forward, a collision bulkhead. The keel is of lead, which weighs about seventy tons, and is placed about three feet lower than is the *Volunteer's*. Her channels and chain-plates are placed outside, as usual on English vessels. The sternpost shows considerable rake, and the bow is a clipper one, and very handsome. She has a reefing bowsprit, which can be shortened six feet.

The sweep of the deck is particularly easy. The covering boards are of teak, and the deck fittings, which are of the same material, are arranged to give the greatest possible space for the handling of the yacht. Her bulwarks are low, mahogany-stained inside, and finished with a neat rail of elm. The companion-way is handsomely finished in teak and mahogany, and the main saloon in American walnut. The latter is very roomy, of the full width of the yacht, is upholstered in cretonne, and is handsomely furnished. A ladies' cabin, aft, is conveniently arranged. Just forward of the main saloon are the officers' rooms and the galley, which, with the forecastle, are well furnished and lighted. The forecastle accommodates twenty men, iron swinging berths being used. The main rigging is of steel, and the jib-halliards are of galvanized iron chain.

Her career up to the time of her sailing for this country eclipsed that of any other British yacht, and was, indeed, remarkable. In her first race, on May 28, 1887, she easily defeated the *Irex* and *Genesta*, and in fifteen races, in the following five weeks, she won eleven first and two other prizes, amounting to over $3,000, defeating all of England's crack yachts. Commanded by Capt. John Barr, of Gourock, Scotland, one of the foremost racing yacht captains of Great Britain, the *Thistle* sailed for America on July 25, the Scotch people confidently believing that she would return with the America's Cup.

The measurements required by the rules of the New York Yacht Club are all that have ever been officially given to the public; but the others, given below, are believed to be correct: —

Length over all, 108.50 feet; length on water-line, 86.46 feet; beam, about 20.35 feet; draught, about 13.80 feet;

length of mast, from deck to hounds, about 62 feet; length of top-mast, about 45 feet; length of boom, about 80 feet; length of gaff, about 50 feet; length of bowsprit, outboard, about 38 feet; length of spinnaker-boom, about 70 feet; ballast, about 70 tons; displacement, about 138 tons; sail area (New York Yacht Club rules), 8,968 square feet; racing measurement (New York Yacht Club rules), 89.20.

THE TRIAL RACES OF 1887.

On September 13, the first of the trial races of American sloops was started over the New York Yacht Club inside course. The only entries were the *Volunteer*, centre-board sloop, Boston, and the *Mayflower*, centre-board sloop, New York. During the season the spar-plan of the *Mayflower* had been slightly altered.

After the yachts had started the wind subsided, and a postponement was made.

On September 15 another attempt was made to have the trial, but the boats did not start, owing to a lack of wind.

The next trial race, which proved to be the decisive one, was sailed on September 16, over an irregular course, starting from the Scotland Lightship. The mark-buoys were so placed as to give the yachts all kinds of sailing. The wind was strong from the north-west by north, and the boats were given a ten-mile run south-east by south, then a nine-mile leg west-south-west; thence back to the first mark, and a beat back to the starting-point; distance, 38 miles. On only one leg did the *Mayflower* outsail the *Volunteer*, and then only by 22 seconds. The *Volunteer's* performance satisfied the committee that another trial was not necessary.

THE SUMMARY OF THE RACE.

Course. — 38 miles; 10 miles, south-east by south, starting from Scotland Lightship; thence 9 miles, west-south-west; thence back, around the first mark, to the starting-point.

Wind. — Varying from 8 to 12 miles an hour; north-west by north.

	Start.	First Mark.	Second Mark.	Third Mark.	Finish.	Elapsed Time.
	H. M. S.	H. M. S.	H. M. S.	H. M. S.	H. M. S.	H. M. S.
Volunteer	11 11 57	12 17 43	1 03 23	1 50 32	3 32 46½	4 20 49¼
Mayflower	11 14 43	12 20 07	1 07 10	1 56 18	3 51 34⅗	4 36 51¼

The *Volunteer* defeated the *Mayflower* 16 minutes 2⅖ seconds, elapsed time.

The committee immediately decided that the *Volunteer* was the better all-around boat, and notified General Paine that she had been selected to sail against the *Thistle* for the Cup.

THE CUP RACES OF 1887.

The First Race, Tuesday, September 27. — The first of the great Cup races of 1887 occurred on Tuesday, September 27, and was sailed over the inside course. The excitement over the event was even greater than that over the two previous contests for the Cup, and there was a strong feeling of doubt as to the result, owing to the splendid record of the *Thistle* and to the secrecy in regard to her model. It was a struggle between the fleetest yachts which Great Britain and America had ever produced, and the hundreds of steam and sailing craft which were massed about the starting-point, ready to chase the racers, formed a picture which was beautiful in the extreme. The contest was closely followed, not only by the people of this country, who eagerly watched the bulletins of the race, but by the people all over the British Isles, where the excitement ran high. The *Thistle* had shown that she was best adapted to a light wind, and, as that was the kind of a breeze in which the race was started, a close contest was looked for.

After waiting two hours for the wind to freshen, the first signal gun was fired at 12.20 o'clock, and the racers, with main-sails, club-top-sails, forestay-sails, jibs, and jib-top-sails set, played about the line, each trying to secure the more advantageous position. The *Thistle* was the first to cross, at 12:33:06, and went over on the port tack, close up to the windward end of the line, — the wind then being light from the southward. The *Volunteer* followed directly in her wake, and crossed on the same tack at 12:34:58¼ o'clock. The moment the beautiful white sloop crossed she began to close up the gap of five hundred feet which existed between them, and as she overhauled her rival cheer after cheer burst from the thousands of spectators. The *Thistle* was being held close to the wind, but just before the *Volunteer* reached her she went about on the starboard tack and headed for the Bay Ridge shore. The *Thistle's* skipper evidently believed that the *Volunteer* would blanket him, and he made the tack, in the hope that the sloop would follow him and thus be under his lee. The *Volunteer*, however, kept on her course. On this tack the *Thistle* drew out of the wind and into the strong tide, and as the *Volunteer* was holding the breeze well, the cutter again went about and stood over toward her. At 12.47 o'clock the *Volunteer* tacked to starboard, crossed the *Thistle's* bow, and held the weather position. It was a move which served to firmly fix the belief in the sloop, and it was heartily applauded. The *Volunteer* now seemed to get a stronger breeze and increased her pace, while the *Thistle* sailed lazily, and with her sails hardly filled. At half an hour from the start the *Volunteer* had a lead of more than an eighth of a mile, and at buoy 13 she was fully a half-mile to the fore. Not only was she drawing away, but she was pointing higher into the wind than the cutter. For a short time after this the wind shifted and decreased somewhat in force, both boats faring alike; but it soon increased, and the *Volunteer* was the first to get the benefit. At buoy 10 the sloop led the cutter by over a mile, and was much farther to windward. She passed the buoy at 2:21:03, and the *Thistle* did not round until 2:36:45 o'clock.

The second quarter of the course — from buoy $8\frac{1}{2}$ to the Sandy Hook Lightship — was a reach of about ten miles, and the *Volunteer* made it on a long starboard tack. She rounded the lightship at 3:42:12, having added over three minutes to her lead since leaving buoy 10. She made a splendid homeward run, meeting the *Thistle* about a mile and a quarter from the lightship. The latter was rounded by the Scotch boat at 4:01:15 o'clock. At buoy $8\frac{1}{2}$ the *Volunteer* broke out her spinnaker, and proudly sailed up the last stretch of the course, with the grandest convoy of steam vessels that ever accompanied a yacht. The finish line was reached at 5:28:$16\frac{1}{4}$ o'clock, and then there arose a din of congratulation which could not be excelled. The *Thistle's* homeward run was her best work of the day. Under her enormous silk spinnaker, which almost hid her hull, she gained one minute and twenty-six seconds on the *Volunteer*, from the lightship to the finish line. She was a badly-beaten boat, but the demonstration in her honor, at the end of the race, was as grand as the one to the victor.

THE SUMMARY OF THE RACE.

COURSE. — 38 miles; New York Yacht Club inside course.

WIND. — Average force about 8 knots an hour; south at the start, then west, backing to south-west during the first half of the race, and south-east during the remainder.

	Start.	Buoy 10.	Sandy Hook Lightship.	Finish.	Elapsed Time.	Corrected Time.
	H. M. S.	H. M. S.	H. M. S.	H. M. S.	H. M. S.	H. M. S.
Volunteer	12 24 58¼	2 21 03	3 42 12	5 28 16¼	4 53 18	4 53 18
Thistle	12 33 06	2 36 45	4 01 15	5 45 52¼	5 12 46¼	5 12 41¾

The *Volunteer* defeated the *Thistle* by 19 minutes 23¾ seconds, corrected time.

The *Volunteer* allowed the *Thistle* 5 seconds.

On Thursday, September 29, the day set for the second race, the wind was so light that the yachts did not start.

THE SECOND RACE WAS SAILED ON SEPTEMBER 30, the course being twenty miles to windward, starting from the Scotland Lightship, and back to the starting-point. The wind was east by north, blowing at the rate of twelve knots an hour, and as it was raining, and there was a good sea on, the yachts had a fine opportunity to show their abilities in heavy weather. The manœuvres for position at the start resulted in the *Volunteer* getting the advantage. The *Thistle* went over the line at 10:40:21, and the *Volunteer* at 10:40:50¾, the latter being on the weather quarter of the cutter. The outer mark-boat was stationed east by north, twenty miles distant, and both yachts started off for it on the starboard tack. With sails trimmed flat and rigid as boards, the yachts rushed almost bow and bow through five or six miles of the heavy sea, and made a beautiful race. They were both jammed close to the wind, but the *Volunteer* could hold herself higher than her rival, and during this tack she crept foot by foot to windward of the Scotch boat, although not outfooting her. At 11.48 o'clock the *Thistle* went about on the port tack, she then being well in toward the Long Island shore. The *Volunteer* continued on her course, and crossed the bows of the cutter with fully five minutes to spare. Such was her gain in the first hour and a quarter of the race. The sloop tacked to port at 1:51:40 o'clock, and both stood off on this tack for an hour, during which the Boston boat continued to draw up to windward more than did the visitor. The *Thistle* went about on the starboard tack at 12.51, and the *Volunteer* followed at 1.10 o'clock. Fifteen minutes later the latter set her club-top-sail over the gaff-top-sail and soon split tacks, standing out to sea, while the *Thistle* kept on along the shore. But one more tack was necessary, and the sloop accordingly, at 2.20 o'clock, tacked to starboard, and began her run to weather the outer mark-boat, which was a mile away. She rounded the mark at 2:26:40½ o'clock, and it was not until 2.41

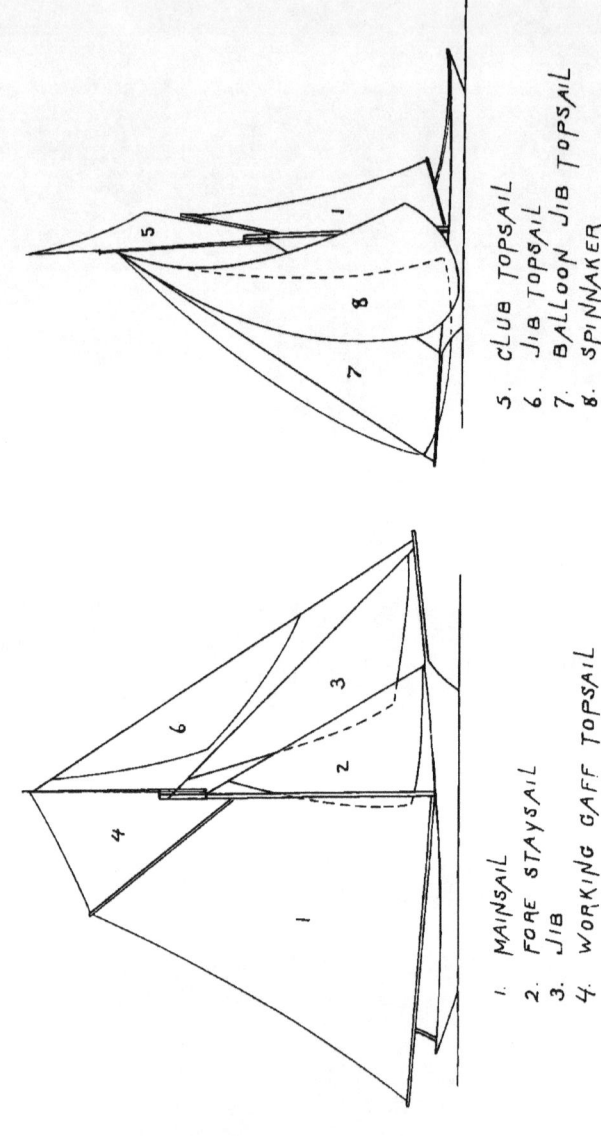

DIAGRAM OF SAILS.

o'clock that the *Thistle* reached the same point. The *Volunteer* had beaten the *Thistle* nearly fifteen minutes in their twenty-mile race to windward. The sloop's spinnaker was set with great caution, and she was soon bowling along with that and her main-sail, club-top-sail, and balloon jib-top-sail. Immediately after rounding, the *Thistle's* balloon jib-top-sail and spinnaker were set, the latter, as was the *Volunteer's*, being to port. Here the cutter showed her running powers, and went along at a pace which was faster than the sloop's, although she could not overhaul the latter. In the run of twenty miles before the wind, her gain was two minutes fifty-four and one-half seconds. When four miles from the finish line the *Thistle* took in her spinnaker; the *Volunteer*, a mile ahead, also taking in hers at the same time. In these relative positions the racers bore down on the lightship, both being on the port tack.

The *Volunteer* crossed the line at 4 : 23 : 47, and the *Thistle* at 4 : 35 : 12 o'clock. The Boston sloop had won the race, and was proclaimed the winner of the America's Cup, while cannons and steam whistles rent the air, and cheer after cheer added to the tumult.

THE SUMMARY OF THE RACE.

COURSE. — 40 miles; 20 nautical miles to windward, starting from Scotland Lightship, and returning to the starting-point.

WIND. — Average force, 14 knots an hour; east by north at the start, then hauling to east-south-east and backing to east.

PAINE-BURGESS TESTIMONIAL.

	Start.	Outer mark.	Finish.	Elapsed Time.	Corrected Time.
	H. M. S.	H. M. S.	H. M. S.	H. M. S.	H. M. S.
Volunteer	10 40 50¾	2 26 40½	4 23 47	5 42 56¼	5 42 56¼
Thistle	10 40 21	2 41 00	4 35 12	5 54 51	5 54 45

The *Volunteer* defeated the *Thistle* by 11 minutes 48¾ seconds, corrected time.

The *Volunteer* allowed the *Thistle* 6 seconds.

CONTESTS FOR THE CUP.

RECORD OF THE STRUGGLES IN AMERICAN WATERS. — Since the America's Cup came into the custody of the New York Yacht Club there have been seven contests for it, as follows: —

FIRST CONTEST.
1870.   Winner.   Loser.
Aug. 8 . . American schooner Magic . . . British schooner Cambria.

1871.   SECOND CONTEST.
Oct. 16 . . American schooner Columbia . . British schooner Livonia.
Oct. 18 . . American schooner Columbia . . British schooner Livonia.
Oct. 19 . . British schooner Livonia . . . . American schooner Columbia.
Oct. 21 . . American schooner Sappho . . . British schooner Livonia.
Oct. 23 . . American schooner Sappho . . . British schooner Livonia.

1876.   THIRD CONTEST.
Aug. 11 . . American schooner Madelaine . . Canadian schooner Countess of Dufferin.
Aug. 12 . . American schooner Madelaine . . Canadian schooner Countess of Dufferin.

1881.   FOURTH CONTEST.
Nov. 9 . . American sloop Mischief . . . . Canadian sloop Atalanta.
Nov. 10 . . American sloop Mischief . . . . Canadian sloop Atalanta.

1885.   FIFTH CONTEST.
Sept. 14 . . American sloop Puritan . . . . British cutter Genesta.
Sept. 16 . . American sloop Puritan . . . . British cutter Genesta.

1886.   SIXTH CONTEST.
Sept. 7 . . American sloop Mayflower . . . British cutter Galatea.
Sept. 11 . . American sloop Mayflower . . . British cutter Galatea.

1887.   SEVENTH CONTEST.
Sept. 27 . . American sloop Volunteer . . . Scotch cutter Thistle.
Sept. 30 . . American sloop Volunteer . . . Scotch cutter Thistle.

THE AMERICA'S CUP

AND

NEW DEED OF GIFT TO THE NEW YORK YACHT CLUB.

THE AMERICA'S CUP

AND

NEW DEED OF GIFT TO THE NEW YORK YACHT CLUB.

THE AMERICA'S CUP.

The America's Cup, erroneously called the Queen's Cup, is the one-hundred-guinea cup given by the Royal Yacht Squadron of England to be competed for by yachts of all nations. It was the first international trophy ever offered, and is emblematic of the yachting supremacy of the world. It was won by the schooner-yacht *America* at Cowes, England, Aug. 22, 1851, and has been retained in this country ever since. It is of solid silver, and elaborately ornamented, standing fully two feet high and weighing at least one hundred ounces. Around its broadest part are medallions, variously inscribed. The first is as follows: "One Hundred Guinea Cup, won August 22, 1851, at Cowes, England, by yacht *America*, at the Royal Yacht Squadron Regatta, open to all nations, beating — " and then follows the names of all the vessels which started in the race. On the next medallion is engraved: "Schooner *America*, 170 tons, Commodore J. C. Stevens: built by George Steers, New York, 1851." On the other medallions are inscribed the records of the other races for the Cup.

As stated earlier in these pages, the Cup became the property of the *America's* owners, and was held by them until July 8, 1857, when it was given to the New York Yacht Club. The Club retained it until November, 1881, when it was surrendered by them to the sole survivor of the former owners. Mr. George L. Schuyler, and by him regranted to the Club, January 4, 1882, on new conditions. These conditions have been amended the present year by what is called the new deed of gift from Mr. Schuyler to the Club.

THE NEW DEED OF GIFT AND CHALLENGE RULES.

GEORGE L. SCHUYLER, the sole surviving owner of the America's Cup, made a new deed of gift of the Cup, in October, to the New York Yacht Club, and at a regular meeting of the club, October 27, 1887, the deed was read as follows: —

This deed of gift, made Oct. 24, 1887, between George L. Schuyler, as sole surviving owner of the Cup won by the yacht *America* at Cowes, Eng., Aug. 22, 1851, of the first part, and the New York Yacht Club, of the second part, witnesseth:

That the said party of the first part, for and in consideration of the premises and the performance of the conditions and agreements hereinafter set forth by the party of the second part, has granted, bargained, sold, assigned, transferred, and set over, and by these presents does bargain, sell, assign, transfer, and set over unto said party of the second part, its successors and assigns, the Cup won by the schooner-yacht *America* at Cowes, Eng., upon Aug. 22, 1851, to have and to hold the same to the

PAINE-BURGESS TESTIMONIAL.   89

said party of the second part, its successors and assigns, in trust, nevertheless, for the following uses and purposes : —

This Cup is donated upon the condition that it shall be preserved as a perpetual challenge Cup for friendly competition between foreign countries. Any organized yacht club of a foreign country, incorporated, patented, or licensed by the Legislature, Admiralty, or other executive department, having for its annual regatta an ocean water-course on the sea, or on an arm of the sea, or one which combines both, shall always be entitled to the right of sailing a match for this Cup with a yacht or vessel propelled by sails only and constructed in the country to which the challenging club belongs, against any one yacht or vessel constructed in the country of the club holding the Cup.

The yachts or vessels, if of one mast, shall be not less than sixty-five nor more than ninety feet on the load-water line; if of more than one mast, they shall be not less than eighty feet nor more than one hundred and fifteen feet on the load-water line.

The challenging club shall give ten months' notice in writing, naming the days for the proposed races, but no race shall be sailed on the days intervening between November 1 and May 1.

Accompanying the ten months' notice of challenge there must be sent the name of the owner and a certificate of the name, rig, and following dimensions of the challenging vessel, namely: Length on load-water line, beam at load-water line, and extreme beam, and draught of water, which dimensions shall not be exceeded; and a Custom-House registry of the vessel must be sent as soon as possible.

Vessels selected to compete for this Cup must proceed under sail on their own bottoms to the port where the contest is to take place.

Centre-board or sliding-keel vessels shall always be allowed to compete in any race for this Cup, and no restriction or limitation whatever shall be placed upon the use of such centre-board or sliding keel, nor shall the centre-board or sliding keel be considered a part of the vessel for any purposes of measurement.

The club challenging for the Cup and the club holding the same may, by mutual consent, make any arrangement satisfactory to both as to the dates, courses, number of trials, rules, and sailing regulations, and any and all other conditions of the match, in which case also the ten months' notice may be waived.

In case the parties cannot mutually agree upon the terms of a match, then three races shall be sailed, and the winner of two of such races shall be entitled to the Cup. All such races shall be on ocean courses, free from headlands, as follows: —

The first race, twenty nautical miles to windward and return; the second race, an equilateral triangular race of thirty-nine nautical miles, the first side of which shall be a beat to windward; the third race, if necessary, twenty nautical miles to windward and return, and one week-day shall intervene between the conclusion of one race and the starting of the next race.

These ocean courses shall be practicable in all parts for vessels of 22 feet draught of water, and shall be selected by the club holding the Cup; and these races shall be sailed subject to the rules and sailing regulations, so far as the same do not conflict with the provisions of this deed of gift, but without any time allowance whatever.

The challenged club shall not be required to name its representative vessel until at the time agreed upon for the start; but the vessel when named must compete in all the races, and each of such races must be completed within seven hours.

Should the club holding the Cup be, for any cause, dissolved, the Cup shall be transferred to some club of the same nationality eligible to challenge under this deed of gift to trust and subject to its provisions.

In the event of the failure of such transfer within three months after such dissolution, said Cup shall revert to the preceding club holding the same, and under the terms of the deed of gift.

It is distinctly understood that the Cup is to be the property of the club, subject to the provisions of this deed, and not the property of the owner or owners of any vessel winning a match.

No vessel which has been defeated in a match for this Cup can be again selected by any club as its representative after a contest for it by some other vessel has intervened, or until after the expiration of two years from the time of such defeat.

And when a challenge from a club fulfilling all the conditions required by this instrument has been received, no other challenge can be considered until the pending event has been decided.

And the said party of the second part hereby accepts the said Cup, subject to the said trust, terms, and conditions, and hereby covenants and agrees, to and with the said party of the first part, that it will faithfully and fully see that the foregoing conditions are fully observed and complied with by any contestant for the said Cup during the holding thereof by it, and that it will assign, transfer, and deliver the said Cup to the foreign yacht club whose representative yacht shall have won the same in accordance with the foregoing terms and conditions, provided the said foreign club shall, by instrument in writing, lawfully executed, enter with the said party of the second part into the like covenants as are herein entered into by it, such instrument to contain a like provision for the successive assignees to enter into the same covenants with their respective assignors, and to be executed in duplicate, one to be retained by each club, and a copy thereof forwarded to the said party of the second part.

In witness whereof said party of the first part has hereunto set his hand and seal, and the said party of the second part has caused its corporate seal to be affixed to these presents, and the same to be signed by its Commodore and attested by its Secretary, the day and year first above written.

GEORGE L. SCHUYLER,
THE NEW YORK YACHT CLUB,
By ELBRIDGE T. GERRY,
Commodore.
JOHN H. BIRD,
Secretary.

{ Seal of the New York Yacht Club. }

In the presence of H. D. HAMILTON.

After the reading of the new deed, the following resolution was unanimously passed: —

Resolved, That the New York Yacht Club accepts the Cup won by the schooner-yacht *America*, upon the terms and conditions stated in the deed of gift executed and delivered by George L. Schuyler as surviving owner thereof to it, bearing date the 25th day of October, 1887, and hereby testifies and confirms the acts of the Commodore and Secretary of this club in joining in the execution and acceptance of said deed of gift.

Resolved, That the deed of gift of the America's Cup be entered at length upon the minutes of this club, and that the Secretary be and is hereby requested to furnish to all foreign yacht clubs a copy thereof.

BIOGRAPHICAL SKETCHES

OF

CHARLES J. PAINE AND EDWARD BURGESS.

BIOGRAPHICAL SKETCH

OF

CHARLES J. PAINE.

CHARLES JACKSON PAINE was born in Boston in the year 1833, being the eldest of three brothers, — Charles J., William C., and Robert T. He has three sisters, all unmarried. His brother William, whose country residence is at Beverly Farms, graduated at the head of his class in Harvard University, and subsequently left West Point number one in his class. He was in the army but a short time. Robert T. is well known for his interest in all philanthropical and public movements. Charles Jackson Paine's name is borne upon the list of graduates of Harvard University in the year 1853; among his classmates being such men as John Quincy Adams, Albert Gallatin Browne, Uriel H. Crocker, Elbridge Jefferson Cutler, Wilder Dwight, Charles W. Eliot, Arthur Theodore Lyman, Robert S. Rantoul, John D. Washburn, Aaron D. Weld, and Justin Winsor. Mr. Paine studied law, and is still recognized as a lawyer by profession; but it does not appear that he has ever practised. He inherited a modest property, and upon his marriage with a daughter of the late John Bryant he found his belongings very considerably increased. The father of his bride was the senior member of the old mercantile firm of Bryant & Sturgis, whose operations began in dealings with the North American coast and up the Columbia river, and entering later into the East India trade. General Paine has given his attention chiefly to large railway enterprises, and being one of those favored ones who possess the Midas touch, his operations have universally proved successful.

General Paine's war record is an honorable one. He was commissioned as captain in the Twenty-Second Massachusetts Infantry (the Henry Wilson regiment), Oct. 8, 1861, and remained with it until the following January, when he resigned to accept higher office elsewhere. During his connection with the Twenty-Second he saw no active service, the corps being within the defences of the capital through the winter of 1861-62. But while in this camp of instruction Captain Paine received a valuable training in military affairs, under the instruction of a competent teacher, Col. Jesse A. Gove, who, it will be remembered, was killed at Gaines's Mill, June 27, 1862. Gen. Nelson A. Miles was a lieutenant in the Twenty-Second, also Gen. Thomas Sherwin. On the 14th of January, 1862, Captain Paine was promoted to major of the Thirtieth Massachusetts, Lieutenant-Col. Jonas H. French being in command. This was one of the two Butler regiments over the regularity of whose enlistment there was so much contention between General Butler and Governor Andrew. Major Paine never received his commission from Massachusetts, although it was known that Governor Andrew would have given it had a list of the regiment's officers been forwarded, as directed. With the exception of Colonel

French, who was made aide-de-camp on Butler's staff, and subsequently provost-marshal at New Orleans, the officers of the regiment received their commissions after Colonel Dudley took command. Major Paine remained with the regiment a short time at Ship Island, and then returned to Massachusetts. After the occupancy of New Orleans, General Butler opened recruiting offices in this city, and two white regiments were raised, respectively known as the First and Second Louisiana Infantry.

Major Paine was commissioned as colonel of the Second Louisiana regiment, Oct. 25, 1862. He had previously been commissioned as major of the Thirty-Ninth, but his commission was never issued. Upon receiving notice of his appointment as colonel of the Louisiana regiment, he started from Boston within twenty-four hours, taking the first steamer leaving for New Orleans. He remained with the regiment until March 8, 1864, when he resigned. Colonel Paine went through the war, ending with the capture of Port Hudson, where he commanded a brigade, and where he was severely wounded. On the 4th of July, 1864, he was made a brigadier-general of volunteers, and assigned to the command of the colored division of the Tenth Corps, and took part in both attacks upon Fort Fisher. It was " for meritorious and valuable services " at the capture of that fortress that he received the brevet rank of major-general of volunteers, Jan. 15, 1865. During the closing months of the war he served in North Carolina under Terry and Scoville.

General Paine began his yachting career when he was quite young. He has been a close student in all that pertains to yacht designing and yacht sailing, and Mr.

Edward Burgess says that many of the changes on the *Mayflower* from the *Puritan* were made at the suggestion of General Paine. In yachting circles all over the country, and indeed all over the civilized world, General Paine is well known, and it is generally conceded that he has no superior among the amateur yachtsmen. When General Paine bought the *Halcyon*, ten years ago, she was comparatively a slow vessel. Under his control she was greatly improved, so that during the last few years she was rated even with *Grayling* and *Montauk*. General Paine has a fine summer residence at Weston, Mass., and here he spends much of his time farming, when not on his yacht. General Paine was one of the syndicate which built the *Puritan*, and he was also a member of the executive committee which had charge of her in the season of 1885. After the races the *Puritan* was sold by auction in New York, and she was purchased by General Paine for $13,500. Late in the fall General Paine sold the *Puritan* to Commodore Forbes, and in the following spring he decided to build the *Mayflower*. The *Volunteer*, his latest possession, was built during the present year. Its achievements are too well known to need comment in this place.

General Paine probably is the least known man for one who is so well known that can be found in the descendant of a family which includes a signer of the Declaration of Independence, Robert Treat Paine; the possible author of that immortal document, Thomas Paine; and the writer of that pathetic song "Home, Sweet Home," known everywhere where there are homes, John Howard Payne; — a wealthy citizen, a distinguished military hero, a

yachtsman beyond compare, and yet known personally by
a mere handful. That early ancestor, Hugh de Pajen, of
crusading times, might pass through Boston and be recognized by nearly as many citizens as his descendant of
the nineteenth century.

BIOGRAPHICAL SKETCH

OF

EDWARD BURGESS.

EDWARD BURGESS is a member of one of the best known of Boston families, and was born in this city in 1848. His father was well known as one of the largest traders in West India goods in the East. He developed a fondness for yachting as long ago as 1858, when he began preparations for entering Harvard College, and his interest in the pastime has steadily increased through all the years he has followed it. He graduated at Harvard, in 1871, in the class with Henry Cabot Lodge and other well-known Massachusetts men. Although mathematics was always a favorite study with Mr. Burgess, he did not begin to apply it to naval architecture until 1882, and his first big venture was with the *Puritan*. Among the vessels he has designed may be mentioned the cutter *Rondina* ; centre-board sloops *Puritan, Mayflower, Vandal, Titania,* and *Volunteer;* cutters *Zigeuner, Pappoose;* schooners *Sachem, Gundred;* steam yachts *Hanniel, Sheerwater;* and the flying fisherman, that has recently been launched, called *Carrie E. Phillips.* Notwithstanding his success with the *Puritan,* Mr. Burgess felt confident, after

Edward Burgess

his experience with the winner of the Cup, that he could improve on her lines and make a better "all-round ship"; and as the result of his efforts the *Mayflower* was constructed in 1886, and her superiority over the *Puritan* proved the correctness of his calculations. But the experience of the year 1887 has shown that he is still able to improve upon his own work, for in the *Volunteer* he eclipsed his former efforts, and produced a boat superior in all respects to both the *Puritan* and the *Mayflower*.

Ever since the formation of the Eastern Yacht Club Mr. Burgess has been one of its most active members, and is to-day its secretary. Mr. Burgess has been secretary of the Boston Society of Natural History for fifteen years, but has recently resigned this office from lack of time.

His remarkable achievements thus far in designing the three famous boats to defend the America's Cup in the international regattas have won for him a world-wide reputation, and entitle him to a foremost position as a naval architect and designer of fast vessels.

THE RECEPTION IN FANEUIL HALL.

THE RECEPTION IN FANEUIL HALL.

As soon as the result of the races was ascertained, and it was known that the *Volunteer* had triumphed over her rival the *Thistle*, Mayor O'BRIEN, with his accustomed forethought and public spirit, conceived the idea of tendering a public reception to our fellow-citizens, Messrs. PAINE and BURGESS, who had attained so much distinction on account of their identity with the winning boats in three successive contests for the possession of the America's Cup. It is needless to state that the proposition of His Honor the Mayor met with immediate approval; a committee of arrangements was organized, consisting of the following named gentlemen, to have charge of the reception, and Faneuil Hall was selected as the place where it should be held.

COMMITTEE ON RECEPTION.

CHARLES A. PRINCE,	E. B. HASKELL,
PHINEAS PIERCE,	J. H. HAINES,
HENRY R. REED,	JOHN H. HOLMES,
GODFREY MORSE,	GEO. F. BABBITT,
AUGUSTUS P. MARTIN,	ALBERT T. WHITING,
M. M. CUNNIFF,	HORACE T. ROCKWELL,
W. B. CLAPP,	JOHN S. DAMRELL,
CHARLES H. TAYLOR,	MARTIN BRIMMER,

106   PAINE-BURGESS TESTIMONIAL.

Ralph H. White,	Robert F. Clark,
Eben D. Jordan,	Francis Peabody, Jr.,
Eugene V. R. Thayer,	W. F. Weld,
John Boyle O'Reilly,	Robert H. Stevenson,
Thomas J. Barry,	T. Jefferson Coolidge, Jr.,
Patrick J. Donovan,	Chas. C. Jackson,
David F. Barry,	E. H. Clement,
Jacob Hecht,	W. C. Barrett,
Timothy J. Dacey,	Lawrence Tucker,
A. Shuman,	Walter H. French,
Jesse M. Gove,	M. J. Kiley,
J. Malcolm Forbes,	Frank L. Dunne,
Charles V. Whitten,	Moses Merrill,
Patrick Maguire,	F. A. Waterhouse,
Charles M. Clapp,	W. B. McClellan,
Joseph Iasigi,	Henry W. Savage,
Jonas H. French,	Thomas R. Mathews,
Thomas J. Gargan,	Austin C. Wellington.

The Committee met and organized by the choice of Mr. Robert F. Clark as chairman, who selected Mr. Nathaniel H. Taylor to act as secretary, and preparations for the reception immediately commenced and were carried forward with unabated zeal and energy.

The following correspondence took place between Mayor O'Brien and General Paine in relation to the reception:—

Executive Department, City Hall,
Boston, Sept. 30, 1887.

Gen. Chas. J. Paine:—

Dear Sir,— I take great pleasure in tendering to you my hearty congratulations upon the grand victory which the *Volunteer* has won over the *Thistle*.

I can assure you that I echo the sentiment of the citizens of Boston when I say that they are proud of the honor which you have conferred upon this city by winning, for the third successive year, the greatest yachting races ever known.

I feel that it would give our citizens great pleasure to meet you publicly on your return to Boston; I therefore suggest that you and Mr. Burgess accept, in behalf of the City, a public reception in Faneuil Hall as soon after your arrival here as may suit your convenience. I know that our citizens generally would like to take you each by the hand.

Trusting that you will honor us by accepting this invitation, and inform me of the date that would be agreeable to you,

I remain, yours very truly,

HUGH O'BRIEN,

Mayor.

YACHT *Volunteer*, NEW YORK HARBOR,
Oct. 1, 1887.

Hon. HUGH O'BRIEN, *Mayor of Boston:* —

DEAR SIR, — I have the honor to acknowledge the receipt of your flattering invitation to Mr. Burgess and myself to a public reception in Faneuil Hall, and we fully appreciate the great honor you propose.

We shall both be at home after next Wednesday, and beg you will have any date thereafter which may be agreeable to yourself.

I am, sir, with great respect,

Your obedient servant,

CHAS. J. PAINE.

Upon the receipt of General Paine's letter it was determined to hold the reception on Friday, the 7th of October, at 6 o'clock P.M., and the following communications were forwarded to the City Council by the Mayor: —

CITY OF BOSTON, EXECUTIVE DEPARTMENT,
Oct. 3, 1887.

To the Honorable the City Council: —

GENTLEMEN, — Gen. Chas. J. Paine of the yacht *Volunteer*, and her designer, Mr. Edward Burgess, having accepted an invitation to attend a popular reception to be given them at Faneuil Hall, on Friday, Oct. 7, 1887, at 6 o'clock P.M., you are cordially invited to be present.

A printed invitation, giving admittance to the platform, will be sent to each member of the City Council.

Yours respectfully,

HUGH O'BRIEN,
Mayor.

On motion of Alderman ALLEN, the invitation was accepted. Sent down.

The following was received: —

CITY OF BOSTON, EXECUTIVE DEPARTMENT,
Oct. 3, 1887.

To the Honorable Board of Aldermen: —

The undersigned respectfully petitions for the use of Faneuil Hall on Friday, Oct. 7, 1887, at 6 o'clock P.M., for the purpose of holding a public meeting.

HUGH O'BRIEN,
Mayor.

Referred to the Committee on Faneuil Hall, etc.

Later in the session Alderman N. G. SMITH offered an

order, That the use of Faneuil Hall be granted to the Hon. Hugh O'Brien, Mayor, on Friday, October 7th inst., for the purpose of extending courtesies to Gen. Charles J. Paine, the owner of the champion yacht *Volunteer*, and to the designer of said yacht, Edward Burgess, Esq., free of expense.

Passed, under a suspension of the rule.

Later in the session Alderman Lee offered the following : —

Resolved,[1] That the thanks of the City Council are due to Gen. Charles J. Paine and Mr. Edward Burgess for their energy

---

[1] The following acknowledgment was subsequently received by His Honor the Mayor from Messrs. Paine and Burgess, and transmitted to the City Council: —

EXECUTIVE DEPARTMENT,
Nov. 17, 1887.

To the Honorable the City Council: —

GENTLEMEN, — I have the honor to transmit herewith a communication from Messrs. Charles J. Paine and Edward Burgess, acknowledging the receipt of copies of the resolutions recently passed by the City Council concerning the late international yachting contest.

Yours respectfully,
HUGH O'BRIEN,
Mayor.

To His Honor Mayor O'Brien and the City Council of Boston : —

We have received copies of the resolution of the City Council of Boston, adopted Oct. 3, 1887, thanking us for our services in connection with the late international yachting contest, and we beg to express our deep sense of the honor you have been pleased to confer on us by such an unparalleled compliment. We shall cherish with pride during our lives the beautiful copies of the resolution presented to us, and shall transmit them as most treasured mementoes to our children.

We are, very respectfully,
Your obedient servants,
CHARLES J. PAINE,
EDWARD BURGESS.

BOSTON, Nov. 16, 1887.

and progressiveness in promoting the success of international yachting regattas, and for their victories over their English and Scotch competitors for the last three successive years. The victory of the *Volunteer* over the *Thistle* is of local as well as national importance, and the citizens of Boston will ever hold in kindest remembrance Messrs. Paine and Burgess, who made it possible for our city to have such a great honor conferred upon it.

Ordered, That a copy of this resolution be presented to Gen. Charles J. Paine and Mr. Edward Burgess as an expression of the City Council of Boston for the victories of the *Puritan*, *Mayflower*, and *Volunteer*.

The resolve and order were passed unanimously, under a suspension of the rule, and were adopted in concurrence by the Common Council at their meeting October 6.

The numerous details incident to the reception were carefully looked after by the committee, under the direction of the chairman. Invitations were issued to seats upon the platform, and, as usual, the galleries were reserved for ladies. The decorations were in charge of Mr. M. J. Kiley, and all the materials made use of were furnished by courtesy to the city, especially for the occasion. These consisted of flags and streamers, furnished by I. W. Wheeler & Co.; yacht furnishings, etc., from C. C. Hutchinson and Bagnall & Loud. The floral yacht designs were furnished by William E. Doyle and Twombly & Sons.

The people began to assemble long before the hour announced for the meeting, and at 6 o'clock the hall was crowded in every part, and a dense throng were gathered in the square below. So great was the crowd that travel was impeded, and further ingress to the building was practically impossible.

Within the hall, assembled upon the platform, were to be seen a large number of Boston's distinguished and well-known men. Among them were the following: Robert Treat Paine, Phineas Pierce, Godfrey Morse, Edwin B. Haskell, John H. Holmes, ex-Mayor Augustus P. Martin, ex-Mayor Frederic O. Prince, Mayor William E. Russell, of Cambridge, Charles H. Taylor, T. Jefferson Coolidge, Jr., Jonas H. French, Walter H. French, Francis Peabody, Jr., Col. Robert H. Stevenson, Jacob Hecht, Patrick Maguire, Joseph Iasigi, Thomas J. Gargan, Col. Robert F. Clark, William F. Weld, Jr., Charles C. Jackson, Lawrence Tucker, F. H. Waterhouse, W. B. McClellan, Jesse Brown,[1] Com. Henry W. Savage, Dorchester Yacht Club, M. J. Kiley, George H. Richards, Rev. J. P. Bodfish, Eben D. Jordan, C. M. Clapp, Martin Brimmer, George F. Babbitt, E. H. Clement, Moses Merrill, Hon. Charles Levi Woodbury, Gen. N. P. Banks, M. M. Cunniff, W. E. Barrett, John S. Damrell, Eugene V. R. Thayer, T. J. Barry, P. J. Donovan, George P. Chase, William Everett, Commodore Hovey, Col. Thomas R. Mathews, Harry A. M'Glenen, Henry J. Weil, George N. Fisher, Jr., W. Lloyd Jeffries, Henry Buck, L. M. Clark, Robert T. Boit, Rev. E. A. Horton, Charles F. Loring, James Gallagher, New Haven Yacht Club, Col. Henry Walker.

---

[1] Jesse Brown is the only surviving member of the crew of the *America* and is the brother of Capt. Richard Brown, who was commander of the *America*, at the time the Cup was won. He is a veteran of the Mexican war, and also the late Civil war, and was severely wounded in both wars. He resides in Roxbury.

The following description of the appearance of the hall and the decorations is taken from the "Boston Post" of October 8: —

"The public that had been momentarily thickening, both on the floor and in the galleries, took note perforce of this arrangement, and also of those embellishments of the stage upon which the photographer had focussed his camera. Above the great canvas on which the godlike Daniel is seen making his immortal plea for 'liberty and union' stretched a broad band of white bunting, in the centre of which, in large crimson letters, was the word *Volunteer*, and on the sides the names of her older and somewhat *passé*, but still fast and dashing, sisters *Mayflower* and *Puritan*. It was easy to imagine that it was of this very bunting that the great orator was speaking as he rolled out in his grand organ tones the noble longing: 'Let my eyes' last feeble and lingering glance behold the gorgeous ensign . . . now known and honored throughout the earth, still full high advanced, its arms and trophies streaming in their original lustre, . . . [and] everywhere, spread all over in characters of living light, blazing on all its ample folds as they float over the sea and over the land, and in every wind under the whole heavens, that . . . sentiment dear to every true American heart,' *Puritan*, *Mayflower*, *Volunteer*, now and forever!

"Against the wall, upon either side of the stage, was a floral *Volunteer*, and the two were engaged in a strenuous contest for a cup of bliss, to be the possession of the winner of the general suffrage as the truest likeness of the illustrious original. The yacht upon the northerly side,

under full sail, was ploughing waves of ivy leaves, crested with foam of cape flowers. Her hull was of white asters, her deck of carnation pinks, her spars and rigging of purple immortelles, and her white sails of cape flowers. She was the pet boat of Twombly & Sons. Her designer and modeller was Mr. J. W. Linnell. She was a thing of beauty and a joy through all her eight feet of length to the veteran yachtsmen who gazed at her. 'See the lines of that hull!' exclaimed one of them to a companion; 'the man who designed that had an eye!' An American eagle, perched upon a stand above the yacht, held suspended from his beak a wreath of laurel. The rival *Volunteer* was about of the same dimensions, and was built by William E. Doyle. She had apparently struck a calm, for her sea of ferns lay smooth and sprayless. Her hull and spars and rigging were composed like those of the pendant yacht, but her deck was of white asters instead of carnation pinks. Upon the main-sail she bore in purple immortelles the significant inscription, '11 min. 48¾ sec.' — the 'size' of the *Volunteer's* second victory over the saucy *Thistle*.

"At the southerly corner of the stage, upon a stand covered with the national colors, stood the America's Cup, — not the celebrated trophy itself, but a magnificent floral representation, by means of which Mr. Doyle, the florist and donor, covered himself with glory. It was four feet in height. The handle was of crimson king carnations, the top of yellow chrysanthemums, the neck and base of white asters, and the bowl of pink asters, with a front of white. Upon this front, in purple immortelles, was wrought 'America's Cup,' and upon the base, 'Defended by the *Volunteer.*' Upon the opposite corner of the stage stood a binnacle containing a handsome compass, — a duplicate of that made by Ritchie for the *Volunteer.* At the side of the binnacle was one of the four peak blocks made by Bagnall & Sons for the winner, which used only three of them. It has a bright metal horseshoe upon its side, inscribed 'Good Luck,' and '*Volunteer* of Boston.' This corner of the stage, as well as the other, was flanked with a small yacht cannon of polished bronze metal, mounted upon a mahogany carriage, — duplicates of those carried by the *Volunteer.* Upon the wall at the back of the stage, between the busts of John Adams and John Quincy Adams, was a *fac-simile* of the Ham nautical clock, which strikes bells instead of hours, in the *Volunteer's* cabin. All of these were presented by C. C. Hutchinson & Co.

"Above the big clock, opposite the platform, were the private signals of General Paine, — a blue field, white diamond, and red cross, — and the yellow signal of the Eastern Yacht Club. From the front of the balconies the flags of the Hull, South Boston, Corinthian, Beverly, Lynn, West Lynn, Dorchester, Bunker Hill, Jeffries, Monatiquit, Quincy, and New Bedford yacht clubs depended and mingled their various hues. Six national flags hung from the ceiling. A portrait against the front of the easterly balcony was draped with the American flag. It is one of the permanent ornaments of the hall, and is a likeness of Robert Treat Paine, General Paine's great-grandfather."

The gathering at Faneuil Hall was a most remarkable one, not only in point of numbers, but in character, in the general good feeling displayed, and the enthusiasm expressed throughout. At intervals during the meeting His Honor the Mayor would call a halt in the speech-making and allow the assembled multitude an opportunity to greet the guests of the evening with a hand-shake. The crowd passed over the platform in single file, and it is estimated that at least seven thousand persons availed themselves of the chance to shake hands with Messrs. PAINE and BURGESS.

The following description of the assembly appeared in the "Boston Herald" of October 8: —

"There was nothing about this meeting so striking, nothing so inspiring, nothing so profitable, to the community as the spirit of genuine American patriotism which pervaded it. It was a grand audience to look at, for it was composed of men. Some were young, some were old, but, looked at from the platform, it was a gathering of voters, — of Bostonians such as Faneuil Hall does not often see. As the long procession of men anxious to congratulate Messrs. Paine and Burgess wound its way along, the critical observer could not help noting its character. It was not a gang such as might be called together on the street by the news of some victory of more or less importance. Not at all. It was as fine a collection of solid, sober American citizens as the old hall ever held.

"The American spirit is not dead, nor is it likely to die. The men who spoke last evening, as men who loved their country, — Horton and Bodfish, Woodbury and the rest of them, — were not applauded for their eloquence, but for their patriotism,—and what a lesson they gave to their enthusiastic hearers!

"Whatever honors Messrs. Paine and Burgess may have received, they will never have one so great as this,— that they have stirred up patriotic sentiment from its depths, and have not only given us something to be proud of, but given new life to the pride every American feels in his country and in his citizenship.

"No one who saw that grand array of men in Faneuil Hall last night will ever forget it. For a lifetime it will be remembered."

A few minutes before 6 o'clock Mayor O'Brien appeared upon the platform, followed by General Paine and Mr. Burgess. Their appearance was the signal for an outburst of cheers and applause such as is seldom heard in the historic old building. When the tumult had subsided, Mayor O'BRIEN stepped forward and spoke as follows:—

MAYOR O'BRIEN'S ADDRESS.

LADIES AND GENTLEMEN: Our programme is a long one, and, as time is precious, my remarks will be very brief. This large and enthusiastic meeting must be very gratifying to our distinguished guests. The battle has been fought and the victory won. All honor to Charles J. Paine for the enterprise, the liberality, and courage which enabled him to come off victorious in three successive contests! All honor to Edward Burgess for the inventive genius and ability he has displayed in modelling, designing, and building yachts that for speed are unsurpassed! All honor to the officers and men who manned the *Puritan, Mayflower*, and *Volunteer!* They deserve the gratitude of the country. We hold the Cup that the *America* won more than a generation ago, and we will continue to try and hold it, against all competitors, for generations to come. The *Puritan*, the *Mayflower*, and the *Volunteer*, with their owner, designer, officers, and crews, will always be gratefully remembered by every citizen who believes in American pluck, American seamanship, and American supremacy. I have now the honor of introducing General Paine.

When General PAINE stepped forward the applause that greeted him lasted nearly a minute, and terminated with three cheers and a tiger for the champion of the America's Cup. He was visibly affected by the heartiness of his reception, and spoke as follows: —

SPEECH OF GEN. CHARLES J. PAINE.

I thank you for this reception, and I thank you still more for the hearty greetings with which you have received us. I have always known that yachtsmen cherished the famous America's Cup, and would make themselves, and would encourage in others, every exertion in its defence. But never till now did I realize how entirely the interest in that Cup had pervaded the community, and how deeply it had become a matter of pride and patriotism to guard it safely.

But this immense gathering here to-night proves how general and how intense the interest is, and how great is the gratification of the community at our success in the late contest; and I assure you that the sense of having contributed what little I could to the gratification of so many of my fellow-citizens is a reward far greater than I expected, and the greatest that is possible. I fear some of you expect me to say something about the races; but all who are interested in yachting have read the details in the papers, and those who are not interested in yachting do not care for them. I wish to say this, however, about the race, that one of the causes that contributed to our victory was the fact that we did not undervalue our antagonist. We prepared, as well as we could, to meet the fastest yacht ever built upon the other side of the Atlantic, — a yacht much faster now than most yachtsmen appreciate.

I wish to take this opportunity to publicly thank Captain Haff and the crew of the *Volunteer*, whom I regret not to see here. They have labored with the utmost zeal, and have done grand work from beginning to end. No better men ever trod a yacht's deck. I wish also to thank publicly the members of the New York Yacht Club for their kindness before and during the races. They did everything in their power to help us, both by their personal assistance and by offering the use of their yachts and their crews. And last, but not least, I wish to thank Commodore Forbes of the *Puritan* for bringing his yacht from Naushon to New York for the purpose of helping us. He brought with him as good a crew as any yacht could wish, and it was a useful and a most kindly act.

Only one thing more. Our friends across the water are now thoroughly waked up to the fact that we have a Cup here that they want very much. That Cup represents a great deal, and they are coming for it every year, and each year better equipped; the contests will become closer year after year. But we may always feel hopeful of a happy result while my young friend Mr. Burgess is ready to bring forward a boat to meet them.

At the conclusion of General Paine's remarks, His Honor the Mayor introduced Mr. EDWARD BURGESS, the great yacht designer, who also received a tremendous burst of applause, and after quiet had been restored he spoke as follows: —

REMARKS OF EDWARD BURGESS.

MR. MAYOR AND FELLOW-CITIZENS: If there are any of my schoolmates here they can tell you that among the studies I most sedulously neglected for the reprehensible pastime of drawing yachts upon the margins of my school-books was the important one of rhetoric. I have had cause on some occasions to regret my lack of diligence in this respect, but never as to-night, when I find myself unable to express how deeply I feel the great honor you do me. To use that hackneyed phrase, "my feelings may be better imagined than described." I beg you to use your imagination generously, and fancy I have thanked you as I ought, rather than as my hesitating tongue finds possible.

And now let me join in the homage you offer to the chief guest of the evening, General Paine. I wish I could tell you how much our yachting prestige is due to him. It is needless for me to say that the world knows no other yachtsman like him, — his achievements show that, — but probably few of you, even among those who are yachtsmen, have any idea what it is to carry through a campaign like that just passed. From the beginning General Paine has thought out the effect of every line, and every detail of construction and rig, and directed all, so as to secure him the possession of the fastest yacht in the world. These large racing sloops are most complicated and delicate machines, and only the most skilful engineer can hope to run them with success. I have been simply his executive officer.

On Mr. Burgess resuming his seat three cheers were called for and given in his honor.

Governor AMES was next introduced by the Mayor, and spoke as follows: —

REMARKS OF GOVERNOR OLIVER AMES.

LADIES AND GENTLEMEN: We meet here to-night as Americans to honor two eminent citizens of Boston, who have shown to the world what Yankee ingenuity and enterprise can do. Massachusetts is proud that she can claim them as her sons, and in her name I congratulate General Paine on his energy, patriotism, and courage, and Mr. Burgess on his genius and scientific acquirements, the combinations of which have enabled them for three succeeding years to win victories that have made every American heart thrill with pride.

Let us, then, give to Gen. Charles J. Paine and Designer Edward Burgess that praise with which our hearts are overflowing, and express to them our confidence that as long as they work together Americans can be sure that on sea, at least, our flag will always be in the fore.

Ex-Mayor FREDERIC O. PRINCE was the next speaker.

REMARKS OF THE HON. FREDERIC O. PRINCE.

MR. CHAIRMAN AND LADIES AND GENTLEMEN: When the hearts of our citizens are stirred by strong emotions, touching matters of general interest, they have been accustomed to come to the Old Hall, and have their sentiments expressed in speech. These walls have resounded again and again to the oratory of the patriot, the statesman, the politician, the philanthropist, the eulogist, and others who have addressed their fellow-citizens upon subjects where they have felt deeply and warmly. There is wisdom in this, as eloquence usually results in action. But our people have never come here before on an occasion like the present. No questions touching political or social affairs interest us to-night. This great assemblage of earnest, enthusiastic, and exultant citizens is gathered to express our appreciation of the skill and energy of our two distinguished townsmen — I am glad to know that they are our townsmen and compatriots — in achieving a great victory, — ay, *three* great victories; victories, as you know, of peace and not of war, which have caused no wounds but those of disappointment to the vanquished, and awakened no harsher feelings than, perhaps, the desire and determination for another friendly contest; but victories, nevertheless, which have reflected honor and credit upon Boston and its people.

The story of these contests has often been told, for they have been the frequent theme of discussion in all those places where our citizens are wont to meet and speak of the things which interest them,— at the clubs, the hotels, the exchange, the broker's board — and, I fear, where the consideration of secular things is not in order. The newspapers have been full of the matter. The story will be retold to-night, but I feel that repetition will not tire you.

You well remember, fellow-citizens, how the gallant yacht *America* crossed the ocean and won the Cup of honor in a race, not with one boat only, but with a fleet of English boats; and, what is more, that John Bull, who so rarely knows when he is beaten, conceded the victory, claiming, however, if my memory is correct, that if something had happened — if the wind had been stronger or lighter, or the sea smoother or rougher, or the weather hotter or colder — the result might have been different.

You know that the yachtsmen of the old country have been moved since their defeat by the intense desire to get' back the lost trophy, and made in vain many attempts to do so. This feeling was commendable, and showed the true game spirit. These repeated efforts awakened a deep interest in yachting on both sides of the ocean.

Three years ago another and most vigorous effort

was made to recover the coveted prize, and one of the fastest of the English yachts was entered for the race. Our two distinguished friends, — those we honor to-night, — apprehensive that the New York yachts might not be able to defend successfully the Cup, designed and constructed the beautiful *Puritan*, which, after a contest which greatly excited all the yachting world here, won an easy victory over her competitor.

Undisheartened by defeat, the next year another effort for the Cup was made; this time by a gallant and generous yachtsman, who would have borne victory as magnanimously as he bore defeat. He brought with him a boat with a distinguished record in many English races, but General Paine and Mr. Burgess pitted against her another of their wonderful creations, — our peerless *Mayflower*, — which, Camilla-like, "skimmed along the main" with such speed and success that the Cup remained safely in American hands.

Once more into the breach, — another race was demanded, and now the Scot proposed to take a hand in it, and show his English brothers how fields were won. A beautiful specimen of naval architecture — a boat which had beaten every yacht which had been matched against her in English seas; a boat which "walked the waters like a thing of life "— was entered for the silver prize. We all remember the great excitement which the

challenge made here. It was discussed everywhere.
The "coming race" divided with politics public
attention. Our ignorance of the qualities and
measurements of the Scotch boat intensified for
some time the excitement. The yachtsmen here,
and those versed in yachting matters, felt, perhaps,
no alarm as to the result; but those who knew
less — and these embraced, I suppose, most of our
citizens — were anxious, many — I think a good
many — very anxious, for the safety of the Cup.
I am ashamed to say that I was of the latter
class, for I was greatly alarmed. But again our
gallant friends came to the rescue, and showed
themselves equal to the demands of the occasion.
They designed and built another defender, — the
victorious *Volunteer*, — which showed her Scotch
rival that on the *sea* the race is to the swift,
however it may be on land; for the thunders of a
hundred cannons, and the plaudits of thousands of
delighted spectators, soon proclaimed the third
triumph of Paine and Burgess.

We should be grateful to them. We are grateful.
These victories mean something more than mere
sporting success. They mean that the old American
skill in constructing naval craft — the old American
superiority in seamanship — still survives. They
mean the value of thought and study, and perseverance and courage. They mean that mere accident or luck cannot be relied upon to produce

certain desired results in ship construction, but that the perception of true fixed rules of form, and their application to certain conditions, are requisites for the sure attainment of specific ends. They mean that hereafter the reasoning faculty, and not "the rule of the thumb," must be employed when we would glide swiftly over the seas. They mean the elevation of naval architecture from an art to a science.

These victories also mean naval reform; that our war-ships shall hereafter have speed, — one of the most important factors of success in sea-fights, — for the government cannot fail to employ the genius of Mr. Burgess in modelling our national ships.

My five minutes of time are not sufficient to point out all the value of his work, and I shall not attempt to do so. I am glad that our citizens appreciate so fully what he and General Paine have done. I am glad that they feel so generally — let me rather say so unanimously — grateful to them for the honor they have brought to the city.

St. Paul says that "in everything we should give thanks." After his sea-experience, so graphically described in Scripture, he probably knew something about boats, and would doubtless approve our thanksgiving to General Paine and Mr. Burgess if he were here to-night; so let us obey the injunction, and give them our most grateful thanks.

Boston has been sometimes called "the Athens of America." If we resemble the Athenians of old we should give golden crowns, or their equivalent, to the designers and builders of our three naval graces, — the *Puritan*, the *Mayflower*, and the *Volunteer;* for, if I rightly remember my college reading, our prototypes gave such rewards, not only to the victors in sea-fights, but to those who had the best-appointed and swiftest triremes, and managed them most successfully.

Let, therefore, the subscription in behalf of our two friends — which, I understand, has been started by the New York Yacht Club — become a national one, so that the testimonial shall be every way most valuable, and let Boston do its full part.

By the way, I don't know how the honors of these triumphs are to be divided between the two gentlemen; but, if there be any disagreement, I will say, as President Lincoln said, when two of our generals were contending for the glory of a victory which both helped to achieve, " Have no discussion; there is glory to go round so as to give each all that he can want."

Mayor O'BRIEN here read a telegram to the following effect : —

"MARBLEHEAD.

" The *Volunteer* arrived here at 5 o'clock. Crew on their way to Boston in the 'Herald' tug. Will reach there about 7."

The audience were at this point admitted to the platform to shake hands with General PAINE and Mr. BURGESS. After large numbers had availed themselves of the privilege the speaking was resumed.

Dr. WILLIAM EVERETT was next introduced.

REMARKS OF DR. WILLIAM EVERETT.

FELLOW-CITIZENS: I observe that nobody has yet noticed how entirely proper it is that this celebration should be held in Faneuil Hall. You all know American history perfectly well, and so I need not remind you that when the voice of Massachusetts went forth in favor of freedom from Faneuil Hall, the first answer was that of Patrick Henry, speaking in the old House of Burgesses, in Virginia; and it is now to the House of Burgesses that the United States owe their new Declaration of Independence on the sea.

And, in sober earnest, the signers of the Declaration are well represented in yachting. Of three of our Massachusetts signers — Hancock, Gerry, and Samuel Adams — the name has passed from our State, and the memory is getting fainter. But a lineal descendant of Robert Treat Paine owns the *Volunteer*, and a lineal descendant of John Adams owns the *Pappoose*, — not a bad boat in her way.[1]

---

[1] Commodore Gerry, of the N.Y. Yacht Squadron, is a descendant of Elbridge Gerry.

But I wish here to thank our guests for their great achievement in the name of the scholars of the country, — the men of education and study. Mr. Burgess, as you know, was not originally a boat-builder by profession. He was a yachtsman for amusement ; and his favorite pursuit was natural science, in which he learned to perfect himself at Harvard College, and for his devotion to which he is known at this day by scientific men. He is not only scientific himself, but he married into a scientific family.

The time came when the world called upon him to give an account of his favorite pursuit and his favorite sport. It said to him, "We have given you Harvard College and the Natural History Rooms for your workshop, and Massachusetts bay for your playground ; we have not forced you to pursue any of what are called business paths. Now show us what you have to offer us in return for all these gifts we have presented to you." Mr. Burgess met the call. He applied his favorite science to his favorite sport; and he has brought it to that perfection that not only every sportsman, but every business man in the country, acknowledges his triumph.

In the minute that remains to me I will tell you a little about Mr. Burgess's favorite science. Does every one here realize how completely he has taken yacht building out of the sphere of luck, and made it a certainty? Do you know how long it took on the day of the race to prove that the *Volunteer* had beaten the *Thistle?* They had been preparing for the race for six months: the *Thistle* crossed the line; the *Volunteer* crossed the line; and in *sixty seconds* it was seen that the bow of the *Volunteer* was just that little bit nearer the wind which assured the race as won. But about Mr. Burgess's favorite science. It is the science of insects; what the New York "Nation" has recently seen fit to call "insectology." Now, there are many remarkable things about insects; but most of all is their amazing muscular strength, which enables them to get over the ground as no other animals can. This wonderful power of locomotion has been made the subject of a beautiful little poem. Mr. Burgess knows all about these energetic little bodies. He determined to build yachts better and faster than any that ever came from Liverpool or Glasgow. He determined to do so on scientific principles. He brought to bear the knowledge that his insects had taught him in the Natural History Rooms, and I can give you the result in four lines: —

> The Mersey builds her keels of steel;
> The Clyde her keels of flame;
> The Burgess lays no keels at all,
> But he gets there just the same.

The conclusion of Dr. Everett's remarks amused the audience immensely, and he took his seat amidst applause and shouts of laughter.

Hon. HENRY B. LOVERING was the next speaker. He received a hearty greeting.

REMARKS OF HENRY B. LOVERING.

In all our successes, which have been preliminary to the great victory of the other day, it is the ingenuity and ability of such men as Designer Burgess, and the public spirit and the push of such men as General Paine, to which we are indebted for the supremacy of American ideas abroad. Fellow-citizens, I realize that we stand in this hall packed closely as sardines in a box, and it is not my intention to make a long speech. I want to say just this:—

There is a well-founded feeling abroad, at least in my neighborhood, that if the English want to have any chance of beating the American yachts they must conform to and adopt American designs. Thrice have we defeated the best vessels they have brought across the water, built expressly to carry back the Cup, and it is time they felt a wholesome respect for American ideas.

As I heard the complimentary remarks which have been made of General Paine they brought back to me an incident which occurred in Washington at the time another Paine, of Ohio, was running for United States senator, and when, as you will remember, he succeeded the Hon. Mr. Pendleton.

During Mr. Pendleton's last session Senator Voorhees, who is somewhat of a joker in his way, was looking out of the west window, and he saw something which suggested to him a pun. Voorhees never loses such an opportunity, and, turning to Senator Pendleton, who stood near by, he remarked, "Senator, you should have had a supply of St. Jacob's Oil in your campaign."

The Ohio senator, looking puzzled, replied, "Senator Voorhees, I do not exactly catch the point."

Voorhees pointed out of the window at a mammoth sign upon a neighboring fence and read: —

"St. Jacob's Oil conquers pain."

Now, the point is plain. Let those who come over here in the future to wrest the Cup which we have held so many years secure a bottle or two of St. Jacob's Oil.

But, even then, I'm afraid they could not conquer our victorious Paine.

His Honor the Mayor next introduced Rev. E. A. HORTON, who spoke as follows: —

REMARKS OF REV. E. A. HORTON.

LADIES AND GENTLEMEN: It seems a cruel thing to force the speakers between you and the men you want to shake by the hand. That there is in this gathering something that glorifies old Boston you will readily see. It is sometimes said that the old New England is something that is obsolete; but these men you honor to-night are representatives of everything that is thoroughly New England. Their combined achievement has been secured by brains, pluck, public spirit and enthusiasm. As I saw those streams of people passing over the platform I said to my neighbor, Father Bodfish, that their enthusiasm meant something deeper than mere joy in the victory of a yacht. It represented the patriotic feeling our young men are inspired with when anything representing the nation is pitted against any foreign country. It was my fortune to serve in the United States navy during the war, at a time when many brave men went down to heroes' graves. That conglomeration of vessels, hastily gathered, did a grand work, but under vast difficulties. And to-day our navy is wretched; our commerce a shame. The love of the flag is strong in all men who follow the sea. I am glad that the noble crew of the *Volunteer* kept the flag at the front of the fleet. I don't care a snap for stump speakers or for the average newspapers. I began my career as a man; then became a parson, and when I go down to my grave I shall go down as a man. I speak as a citizen; citizens loyal and proud we ought always to be amid professions and business. I want to see the flag respected, as becomes a great country like ours. I was up in Canada a few days ago. Oh, I didn't run away! While talking with a prominent gentleman there he said that he would much rather we had come thirty thousand strong than three hundred. He would be glad if we had taken the country, and made it a part of the United States. I rejoice in the enthusiasm which makes us love the flag of our country, and I rejoice that New England produces much of what makes this nation great and powerful.

Sentiment is the inextinguishable light of man and country. Sentiment kindles the fervor of this occasion. When men are willing to look up and admire, all things are safe. Such a gathering as this means the drawing together of all elements and classes in sympathy and on a high plane of feeling. It enforces the fact that individuals of wealth in our midst are willing to expend their means for national fame and public pride. Let us encourage every noble impulse. In the midst of mercantile greed, political corruption, and material standards, welcome, thrice welcome, whatsoever quickens the heart of unselfish citizenship.

Hon. CHARLES LEVI WOODBURY was the next speaker.

REMARKS OF HON. CHARLES LEVI WOODBURY.

I came here not to talk to you, shipmates, but to honor two men who have done more for the glory of the United States in the last two years than any other two men between the North pole and the Isthmus of Panama. There is a prospect that the Cup will long remain on this side of the Atlantic. We don't propose to give up the ship in despair, or the Cup, while there is a shot left in the locker. I am reminded that thirty years ago the *America* bore away the proud trophy from the yachtsmen across the water. In later years many interesting contests have been held for that trophy, and three times Boston came forward to defend that Cup. Three times has Boston successfully defended the Cup, and to-night the *Volunteer* is riding gracefully in port, and near her is the *America*. A telegram has been read here to-night saying that the crew of the *Volunteer* will soon be here. Now there is something very sympathetic in this. General Paine served in the war for the preservation of the Union under General Butler, the owner of the *America*, and it is of peculiar interest that these two men should own the first and the last vessel that has won the Cup.

The victory just won by the *Volunteer* has again vindicated the American reputation for seamanship and for ship-building. The seven times that American yachts have successfully defended the Cup shows that we are ahead in everything that pertains to nautical affairs. There was a time when our schooners and our frigates were the fastest vessels afloat. That was about the time of the war of 1812. Our clipper ships came later, and they, too, outstripped, in sailing qualities, all craft afloat. When steam came into use our steamers beat the world. Then desolation fell on our carrying trade. Now we have the fleetest yachts that sail the seas; a little superior in hull, sails, and handling to anything yet brought against them. We thank our competitors for having forced our talent to develop their racing capacity. The stern chase of our Island competitors has lasted long, and I know of only one chance for them to gain the lead, — that is, subsidize Mr. Burgess to build them a craft, and inveigle General Paine to sail it for them.

Rev. J. P. BODFISH was next introduced to the audience, and received a warm reception.

REMARKS OF REV. J. P. BODFISH.

I wish to express my grateful thanks to General Paine, Mr. Burgess, and to the crew of the *Volunteer* for the glorious victory they have won. I think I can appreciate all that the victory cost, having been familiar with yachts from boyhood. They were then my familiar playthings. A great many things entered into that struggle. The patriotism, courage, indomitable energy, fidelity in looking after every detail that contributed to win victory, — these are among the things that engaged the attention of these men. The result was a great victory, won by American skill, American perseverance, and American pluck. A light-house keeper was once asked, "What would happen if your light went out?" With a look of astonishment and pain he exclaimed, "My light shall never go out!" So like him I trust we are determined that our light shall never go out, and that we shall remain firm in the determination to keep the trophy our yachtsmen have so fairly won and so long and gallantly defended.

Rev. MINOT J. SAVAGE next addressed the audience.

ADDRESS AND POEM BY REV. M. J. SAVAGE.

I am the only gentleman present, so far as I have been able to observe, who wears a dress-coat. Well, I think nothing is too good for an occasion like this. When I found myself invited to deliver one of twenty or thirty five-minute speeches, it occurred to me that in the end they might grow monotonous, all being delivered on the same theme. I remember a piece of advice given to me by my old professor. He said: "If you write what you think is throughout an admirable sermon, re-write it and tone down some of the parts, so as to give it variety, even if you have to make some parts of it a little poorer." Warned by that advice, I concluded to contribute at least to the variety, even though it should prove that mine were the poorer part referred to by my professor. So I have written a few verses which I thought might be appropriate to this occasion. Their title is "Bostonia Victrix." It is true that is Latin; but then everybody in Boston knows Latin.

Mr. Savage then read the following poem: —

BOSTONIA VICTRIX.

Let Boston wear her honors
  Most modestly to-day,
Here, where she sits securely,
  The mistress of the bay.
We'll be not over-boastful,
  We'll try not to be vain,
And yet we can't help speaking
  Of Burgess and of Paine!

We'll waive the common honors
  We won so long ago —
The lead we took in letters,
  And all the things we know;
Enough for us at present
  That we have come to be,
In spite of "Rule Britannia,"
  The mistress of the sea.

Since some town had to do it,
    And since New York did not,
'Twas left for little Boston
    To build the fastest yacht.
We'll let our sister city
    Help hold the honors up,
And while we proudly drain it
    Her lips may sip the cup.

We love our English sister;
    Yet, since the seas divide,
We love a little better
    The people on this side.
We're very, yes, quite willing,
    She should all Europe beat;
But find our knees refusing
    To bend, e'en at her feet.

The Scotchman's thorny "Thistle"
    Was meant our pride to prick;
He hoped to see us tingle
    E'en to the very quick!
But, in his own side smarting,
    He feels the thrust severe,
While from his eye escaping
    We see one "Volun-*tear*"!

They say we have no navy;
    But since our Boston sent
(By way of New York) Whitney
    To help the President,
We'll rally and stand by him;
    And now the work's begun,
We modestly stand ready
    To show just how it's done.

"America" and "Puritan";
  The "Mayflower" last year;
But Boston still is growing,
  So — here's the "Volunteer"!
And if the plucky Briton
  Still thinks that he can win,
Then let him bring another,
  And we will take that in.

In short, we've learned to like it,
  This cup we won to keep;
And now that we have tasted
  The blue and briny deep,
We here declare our purpose
  To hold all that we gain,
So long as we have Burgess
  Well backed by General Paine!

Gen. NATHANIEL P. BANKS was introduced as the next speaker.

ADDRESS OF GEN. N. P. BANKS.

It is my privilege, Mr. Mayor, in the brief moments allowed me, to speak of one of your distinguished guests, at least, as my neighbor and my comrade in arms. To him it is something more than a cosmopolitan compliment. It is a welcome from the heart of city, state, and nation, for his vindication of American honor where it has been most threatened — the open seas of the world. To his matchless co-worker — Mr. Burgess — who passed from one international conquest to another, rising steadily and easily to greater success as greater demands were made, until competitors and contestants of nations were exhausted, it gives a spontaneous and continental recognition as the master mind and hand at the head of the column of illustrious constructors and navigators of the age. This is not the first meeting I have attended in honor of an American victory on the sea. I remember a magnificent scene in the Massachusetts House of Representatives, in 1851, on the day when the yacht *America* took part in a contest for supremacy in English waters. While we were in the hall of the House the news came from the Old World that the *America* had won the race. Daniel Webster occupied the floor when the news came. The day was that of the celebration of the opening of railway communication between the American States and the Canadian Provinces, and Webster announced the victory which had been won by the *America*, running against the whole fleet of England and Scotland. "The *America* has won," he said. "Like Jupiter among the gods, America is first, and there is no second." The Canadians did not like it; they thought it out of place; but it was just. Now, I come to honor these young men, not so much for what they have done in this victory, with all that belongs to it, and all the joy it inspires, but because it marks the path of national duty and honor. The great governments of the world are moving to the sea. Russia is moving to the sea; so is Germany; and so are even China and Japan. But where is America? Her power is not on the sea. When Mr. Webster spoke the few words I have repeated, the condition of American commerce and American shipping was very different from what it is now. Then, in 1851, or a few years later, we had a larger tonnage than Great Britain, or any other nation on the globe. England was increasing her tonnage every year at the rate of 28 per cent., and the United States hers at the rate of 58 per cent. In 1876, the centennial of the declaration of American independence, the American flag would have covered the majority of the commercial tonnage of the world. But it had been swept from the sea by combinations of other governments against us. They sought to destroy the supremacy of America on the sea. It was to destroy that supremacy that they made war against America. I do not lay the responsibility for that contest on the shoulders of any class of American statesmen. It arose from the jealousy of the older Nations. It was the feeling of England, and of some other governments, perhaps, that America was becoming too powerful on the sea, as she had been on the land.

Now, in this situation we know what we have to do. No one could have been more rejoiced than I was at this victory; but it is for what is to come, and for what must come, that I rejoice. If we go no farther; if we do not accept the responsibilities and duties of the future; if we do not realize the fact that in all ages, and in all parts of the world, seas have been and must be the great media of communication; that on the sea are fought its greatest battles,—all our rejoicing can be but of little consequence. Look back upon our record. It was the success of our whale-ships which drew from Edmund Burke that splendid eulogium on the capacity and spirit of American sailors; it was our Yankee fishermen that captured British privateers in the mouth of the English Channel; it was Fulton who invented the steamship; it was the American clipper-ship that for a brief period monopolized the commerce of the world; it was the yacht *America* that gave information to the people abroad of what we had at home; it was the American *Monitor* upon which all the naval powers of the world have modelled their defences. It was at that period—1851—that the two greatest journals of the world exclaimed, one after the other: "In everything that is valuable, everything that is for human improvement, exhibited in the World's Fair, America is so far ahead that nobody else is in sight." "The time is coming when America shall command the ocean, and both oceans, and all oceans." It is this last victory of the American *Volunteer* that for the moment struck the world breathless. "It points the way that we are going, and such an instrument we are to use." Is there one human being that does not wish it, man or woman, child or grown person? Why is it not done? Because the Americans will not decide *how* it shall be done. With the Lakes above us and the Gulf below, the Atlantic on this and the Pacific on the other coast of the continent, and with no control of the sea, these flags may hang here, but the men of the future will have a hard time to keep their heads above water. The time is coming when the people will demand that our flag shall be restored to its supremacy on the sea. When that time comes America will win the same honors there that she has won on land.

Hon. THOMAS J. GARGAN was next introduced.

REMARKS OF THOMAS J. GARGAN.

We are here to-night to congratulate Mr. Paine and Mr. Burgess for what they have done in maintaining the honor of the American flag upon the sea. Last night I stood on the cliffs overlooking Marblehead harbor and the waters of the bay beyond, expecting to catch a glimpse of the *Volunteer* then expected hourly to reach port. I was in sight of the place where, during the war of 1812, the *Chesapeake* and *Shannon* fought, and as the gallant Lawrence, the Commander of the *Chesapeake*, fighting against overwhelming odds, was struck down, mortally wounded, his last words were, "Don't give up the ship." There was an inspiration in these words to every American sailor; and how they heeded them and retrieved the disaster we have but to recall the names of Hull, Bainbridge, Decatur, Perry, McDonough, and Porter, and their series of brilliant victories upon the seas and the great lakes that made the war of 1812 memorable, and gave us a place and reputation among the nations of the world. The same spirit which animated Lawrence and his compatriots carried the American flag on the whale-ships of New Bedford and Nantucket to the frozen waters of Baffin's Bay, and made the Yankee clipper-ships in the California, Liverpool, and China trade the wonder and the envy of European nations.

In 1860 our commercial marine was second only to that of Great Britain, with every prospect that before another decade our tonnage would largely exceed that of any nation on the globe, but the war of the Rebellion swept our commerce from the seas; yet the spirit of American seamanship survived the ruin of our commercial marine, and the skill and ingenuity saved the nation in more than one emergency. Farragut and Porter and Winslow were worthy descendants of the men of 1812, and the clever way in which the *Kearsarge* sunk the *Alabama*, a British-built ship, armed with British guns, and largely manned by British tars, sent a thrill of exultation to every true American heart.

If we have been despondent at the decadence of our merchant marine and the impotency of our navy, and have chafed at the manner in which the smallest nations of the earth have insulted us with impunity, and deplored our inability to protect the Samoans against the invasion of Germany, because we had not a ship to protect the American flag in waters of the Pacific ocean, we are cheered by these actions of our yachtsmen: we see that our naval architects have not forgotten their cunning, nor our sailors the art of navigation. We rejoice that the people of this great country, great upon the land, realize at length that no nation can be truly great unless she is able to show her prowess upon the sea.

What comes from these victories is not the mere facts that the *Puritan*, the *Mayflower*, and the *Volunteer* have beaten the British yachts opposed to them; but that General Paine and Mr. Burgess have reawakened that spirit of pride in our common country that ought to make us desire to see our nation assert her supremacy, and that she should be powerful upon the sea as well as upon the land.

General Paine and Mr. Burgess deserve our thanks, ay, more than our thanks, — our gratitude, for reawakening this spirit and stimulating our ambition to be the first power on the water.

> "Far as the breeze can bear, the billows foam;
> Survey our empire, and behold our home;
> These are our realms, no limit to their sway;
> Our flag the sceptre all who meet obey."

The speech of Mayor WILLIAM E. RUSSELL, of Cambridge, was as follows:—

This old hall, Mr. Mayor, has often echoed patriotic words. I believe it never has been stirred by a more patriotic impulse than that which has brought here this outpouring of the people to give a royal welcome to sons of Boston, who have honored her with a national triumph. It must be pleasant to them to know that our welcome rings with patriotism, and our honor to them is a renewed pledge of patriotic love and loyalty. If the victory we celebrate was merely that of one boat over another, there would be little cause for this demonstration; but, when it represents the best efforts of two great nations in honorable rivalry on an important field, the contest is a national contest, and the victory a national triumph.

I have not come, sir, to flatter modest men. Nothing I can say can increase or diminish the glory of what they have done, nor change by one iota our estimate of the ability, perseverance, and generosity that have kept our flag still waving over the flag of England. I have come, as one of thousands, to give expression to the feeling of satisfaction and pride in finding that when our country wills, she can; that ability follows resolution to make her victorious, even over the "Mistress of the Seas."

The test of national greatness is not in burdensome, constant preparation, but rather in her capacity, ability, and patriotism to meet the need of the hour, to *become* ready when the call summons her to the contest.

General Paine, you have demonstrated that, in the bitter days of war, in deadly conflict, in the blessed days of peace, in manly rivalry, there is ever ready a *Volunteer* to answer our nation's call, and to carry her to triumphant victory. For this, sir, we thank and honor you.

At the conclusion of Mr. Gargan's remarks, the crew of the *Volunteer* entered the hall,[1] amid the wildest cheering. On reaching the platform they were formally greeted with three cheers, called for by the presiding officer. His Honor then read the following letter from Captain Haff, explaining why he was unable to be present with his men: —

YACHT *Volunteer*,
MARBLEHEAD, Oct. 7, 1887.

To Hon. HUGH O'BRIEN, *Mayor of Boston:* —

DEAR SIR, — On my arrival at Marblehead I received your kind invitation to be present at the reception which is to be

---

[1] The presence of the crew of the *Volunteer* at the reception was, undoubtedly, due to the journalistic enterprise and foresight of the managers of the "Boston Herald." Knowing that the *Volunteer* was expected at Marblehead in the afternoon they chartered a tug, and cruised about in the lower bay, to hail the victor as soon as she appeared. They fell in with her about four o'clock P.M., and took her in tow to Marblehead, as the wind had failed entirely. The crew were taken on board the tug at six o'clock, and were landed at Long wharf at eight o'clock, proceeding immediately to Faneuil Hall.

given to General Paine and Mr. Burgess at Faneuil Hall this evening. I regret that my health is such as will not permit my leaving the yacht to-night; nothing could afford me greater pleasure than to join you in honoring General Paine.

Very respectfully yours,

H. C. HAFF.

The following is a complete list of the crew: Captain, Henry C. Haff; first mate, Charles Kennison; second mate, Harry P. Haff; quartermasters, Charles Johnson and George Conant ; crew, George Smith, Chris Folsom, George Johnson, John Sarlin, Charles Olson, Harry Anderson, Charles Lotman, of the old *Mayflower* crew, George Moberg, Hans Chester, John Beckman, William Lawrence, John Westerland, George Stone, Andrew Anderson; steward, John Hanen; cook, Frank Samdel; assistant cook, Joseph Mayo.

The members of Dahlgren Post (No. 2) of the G.A.R., South Boston, next entered the hall, headed by Captain Bradley and the Grand Army band. Over the detachment floated a banner with the inscription, "The volunteers of '61 welcome home the victorious *Volunteer*, South Boston." The members of the Post having marched upon the platform in double file, Captain Bradley called for three cheers for General Paine and Mr. Burgess, and they were given with enthusiasm. Captain Bradley then said: —

GENERAL PAINE, MR. BURGESS, THE CREW OF THE *VOLUNTEER:* The volunteers of '61, who, on many a bloody battlefield and slippery deck, fought to maintain the Union and uphold the honor of the flag, welcome you, the volunteers of 1887, who, in a friendly contest, have made the proudest nation in the world strike its colors, and have nailed our own colors to the mast.

The comrades then gave three rousing cheers for the gallant commander and crew of the *Volunteer*, and resumed their line of march. There was no more speech-making after this, and the audience again availed themselves of the opportunity to shake hands with General Paine and Mr. Burgess. A few letters of regret were read from those who had been unable to respond to the Mayor's invitation, and afterwards the immense audience slowly dispersed. The music for the occasion was furnished by the Boston Cadet Band, under the leadership of J. Thomas Baldwin. The police arrangements were under the personal supervision of Deputy-Superintendent Joseph R. Burrill, and were admirable in every respect. The officers had a hard task to restrain and control the immense crowd that thronged the building and all the adjoining streets, but they performed their arduous labor with their accustomed faithfulness, and no accident occurred to mar the interest and pleasure of the event. Taken as a whole, the reception was a grand success.

CORRESPONDENCE, ETC.

The following letters and communications were received by Mayor O'Brien, expressive of regret on the part of some who were unable to be present, and all containing hearty congratulations to the distinguished guests of the evening. Most of them were read at the reception, but the others were received subsequently and have not been heretofore published: —

BEVERLY FARMS, Oct. 3, 1887.

To His Honor HUGH O'BRIEN, *Mayor of Boston:* —

DEAR SIR, — I regret that it is not in my power to accept the polite invitation of the City of Boston to attend the popular reception to be given to Gen. Charles J. Paine and Mr. Edward Burgess on Friday, October 7.

Both are my friends, and one of them, General Paine, is my near connection. Proud as I am of their achievement, I own that the General is the only commander I ever heard of who made himself illustrious by running away from all his competitors.

Yours very respectfully,

OLIVER WENDELL HOLMES.

BOSTON, Oct. 6, 1887.

DEAR SIR, — I have the honor to acknowledge your invitation to attend a popular reception to be given to General Paine and Mr. Burgess at Faneuil Hall on the 7th inst. I regret more than

I can express that imperative engagements, which will take me to New York and Washington, will cause me to leave the State as early as Friday, if not before. As a yachtsman of seventeen years' continuous cruising, I should deem it my duty to do all I could to express my gratification, as a patriot, at the success of the efforts of General Paine and Mr. Burgess to maintain the high position that our country holds in relation to nautical architecture and equipment.

But I hold to General Paine a nearer, and, to me, a dearer connection, of high appreciation. He served with me in the very earliest part of the war of the Rebellion, marched with the army of the Gulf, a young officer, daring, efficient, active, cool-headed. He was then a volunteer I appreciated in the service and defence of his country, and I appreciate the *Volunteer* now, in her successful defence of the country's honor. The fact that he arose step by step to high rank, from merit alone, speaks of the efficiency of General Paine as a soldier. In peace no greater successes have followed the efforts of any man.

When a challenge came that the best creation of British skill in nautical architecture, the *Genesta*, was to come here to take away the America's Cup, General Paine, with the patriotism, liberality, and courage of conviction that such challenge could be met, ordered a vessel to be built, and put the design in the hands of Mr. Burgess, because he knew his skill and worth.

The *Puritan* was put afloat, which, after repeated trials, outsailed all American boats; and then, selected by unanimous judgment to meet the *Genesta*, the *Puritan* beat all England, as well as all America.

The following year a new challenge came from England, and General Paine, knowing that all American skill could do had not been done, built, and Mr. Burgess designed, the *Mayflower*, which not only beat all England and America, but beat the *Puritan* beside.

Again, this year, all England being satisfied of our superiority, Scotland supposed that a better boat could be devised and built in her waters than either England or America could produce, and all Scotland's nautical skill was devoted to the construction and equipment of the *Thistle*, which, on trial, beat all England. General Paine believed from the report of these victories that a better boat had been produced than England had sent here before, confident that the resources of American skill in that regard had by no means been exhausted, built, and Mr. Burgess designed, the *Volunteer*, the superiority of which has been demonstrated by her beating not only all the rest of the United States, and all that England could do, but also the *Puritan* and the *Mayflower*, and the Scotch boat *Thistle*, by larger odds than they had theretofore beaten England and America.

You will, my dear Mr. Mayor, therefore appreciate my regrets that I must be away in body, but I shall be present in spirit with everything that goes to show the highest recognition of General Paine, the boat *Volunteer*, and the unequalled skill of Mr. Burgess, the designer of the *Puritan*, the *Mayflower*, and the *Volunteer*, who never permits anybody to outstrip him but himself.

I am, very truly, your friend and servant,

BENJAMIN F. BUTLER.

Hon. HUGH O'BRIEN, *Mayor of the City of Boston.*

BOSTON, Oct. 7, 1887.

The Hon. HUGH O'BRIEN: —

DEAR SIR, — Owing to an absence from the city, your kind invitation is only this moment received, or it would have had a more prompt reply. I regret that my engagement compels me to decline it, as I cordially sympathize in the pleasure afforded by the triumph of the nautical and scientific skill and energy of General Paine and Mr. Burgess. General Paine has aided to render the name of the American Volunteer illustrious, both in peace and war.

With much respect, your obedient servant,

CHARLES DEVENS.

EAST POINT, NAHANT, Oct. 5, 1887.

Hon. HUGH O'BRIEN : —

DEAR SIR.— An imperative engagement, which obliges me to go to New York on Friday, prevents my acceptance of your very kind invitation to take part in the reception to General Paine and Mr. Burgess on that evening.

I regret extremely that this should be the case, for nothing would give me greater pleasure than to be present. I should like to join with the multitude who will be there in expressing to General Paine and Mr. Burgess the pride we all feel both in their victorious talent and skill, and in the simple, manly, and straightforward way in which they have borne themselves as the representatives of the country in their great yachting contests. As it is, I can only send to them my warmest congratulations, and remain, with many thanks to yourself,

Very truly yours,

H. C. LODGE.

NAUSHON ISLAND, Oct. 5, 1887.

His Honor HUGH O'BRIEN, *Mayor of Boston:* —

Mr. J. M. Forbes, Sr., regrets that he cannot avail himself of your polite invitation for Friday evening's meeting at Faneuil Hall. He not having the gift of speech can only express his appreciation of the good work done by General Paine and Mr. Burgess, and his hope that the young and vigorous men who have the subject in hand will take measures to carry into effect the existing public feeling in some substantial and practical manner that is worthy of our Commonwealth and of your city.

JOHN M. FORBES, Sr.

MILTON, Oct. 6, 1887.

SIR, — Referring to your kind invitation for the 7th inst., and my acceptance thereof conditionally, I have to say with regret that my physician absolutely forbids my going to the meeting to-morrow evening. If I could go, I certainly could not in five minutes express all I feel toward Messrs. Paine and Burgess.

I am, very respectfully, your servant,

R. B. FORBES.

CONGRATULATIONS FROM THE OLD COLONY CLUB.

PLYMOUTH, MASS.

General PAINE and Mr. BURGESS: — The Old Colony Club of Plymouth, Mass., sends congratulations.

A. AND M.

MESSAGE FROM THE SONS OF MARTHA'S VINEYARD.

Messrs. CHARLES J. PAINE and EDWARD BURGESS, *Faneuil Hall, Boston, Mass.*: —

GENTLEMEN, — The almost numberless congratulations that you have received of the highest complimentary nature, both through the press and by private communication, must have convinced you how justly proud and heartily appreciative are the American people for your successful efforts in again preserving to them the America's Cup, and how fully your patriotism, genius, and skill are recognized throughout the entire yachting world. So desirous as is every one of acquainting you with their approval, it is scarcely possible to express it without its being a mere repetition.

But at the last meeting of the Sons of Martha's Vineyard it was unanimously conceded that, if the club did not contribute to the meeting to be held in Faneuil Hall in honor of your achievement, a testimonial of their interest in the great international race, and the enthusiasm they felt over its successful conclusion, it would ever after be a matter of disappointment and regret. The intense interest manifested by all members of this club was shared by all people of Martha's Vineyard, who from their earliest days are so identified with yachting and with trials of speed upon the water, that it may almost be regarded as a sport peculiar to that sea-girt isle. In consequence of their enthusiasm, it was most natural that their fancy should imagine an ideal model, so symmetrical in curve and beautiful in form that she would prove a prodigy of speed. But they knew well it would require the masterhand of a genius to design, and the ideal yachtsman to equip and develop her speed, and ardently hoped that this rare combination of powers would be found and combine to convert this ideal into a pleasant reality.

It affords the greatest satisfaction to recognize that this has been accomplished in the *Puritan*, *Mayflower*, and *Volunteer*, and we hereby congratulate Mr. Burgess on such a demonstration of his wonderful skill, and have only the deepest admiration for the patriotism and generosity of General Paine for cheerfully volunteering to defend our trophy from foreign claimants.

In conclusion we confidently say that, as long as these gentlemen continue to exercise their ability in this direction, greater results will yet be attained, and their lofty motive will be emulated by others.

Sons of Martha's Vineyard, by their Committee,

WILLIAM A. MORSE,
WILLIAM H. DAGGETT.
CHARLES DARROW.

NEW BEDFORD, MASS., Oct. 7, 1887.

To Mayor HUGH O'BRIEN, *Faneuil Hall, Boston:* —

At a meeting of the Board of Directors of the New Bedford Yacht Club, held this evening, the following vote was adopted: —

"*Voted,* That this Club is heartily in sympathy with the meeting now being held in honor of Charles J. Paine and Mr. Edward Burgess, and tenders its warmest congratulations."

EDGAR R. LEWIS,
Secretary.

233 CLARENDON STREET, BOSTON, Oct. 4, 1887.

MY DEAR SIR, — It would give me much pleasure if I could accept your invitation and join in doing honor to General Paine and Mr. Burgess; but I have an engagement out of town on Friday, which I find it impossible to change, and therefore I must not hope to be at Faneuil Hall.

I am,
Yours very truly,
PHILLIPS BROOKS.

Hon. HUGH O'BRIEN, *Mayor of Boston.*

HARVARD UNIVERSITY, CAMBRIDGE, MASS., Oct. 4, 1887.

DEAR SIR, — I regret that a previous engagement must deprive me of the pleasure of attending the reception in honor of General Paine and Mr. Burgess, to be given in Faneuil Hall, on Friday, October 7th.

Respectfully yours,
CHARLES W. ELIOT.

Hon. HUGH O'BRIEN.

JAMAICA PLAIN, Oct. 4, 1887.

Hon. HUGH O'BRIEN: —

DEAR SIR, — I am sorry that it will not be in my power to be present in Faneuil Hall on Friday evening and meet General Paine and Mr. Burgess. If I were present I should be glad to express my satisfaction that, though our mercantile marine has been nearly protected out of existence by the War Tariff, and though our navy has disappeared under the weight of the millions appropriated for its maintenance, we have still some Americans who can uphold the credit of our flag on the ocean.

With much respect, yours,
JAMES FREEMAN CLARKE.

The following correspondence, as will be seen, occurred subsequent to the reception, and consists of General Paine's acknowledgment of his appreciation of the honor conferred upon him by the people of Boston, and Mayor O'Brien's letter in reply to General Paine: —

WESTON, MASS., Oct. 10, 1887.

To His Honor MAYOR O'BRIEN, *Boston:* —

DEAR SIR, — I beg you will permit me to express the deep sense of obligation which I feel to you for tendering to Mr. Burgess and myself a reception which was so grand both in its number and its enthusiasm, and which will always remain in my memory as the proudest day of my life. No happiness could exceed that of knowing that I had contributed in some measure to the gratification of so many of my fellow-citizens, and that happiness I feel that I owe to you.

I am, with great respect,
Sincerely yours,
CHAS. J. PAINE.

BOSTON, Oct. 12, 1887.

General CHARLES J. PAINE: —

DEAR SIR, — Your very kind letter has been received. All Boston was so interested in the success of the recent race, that I felt I should fail to represent our glorious old city if I did not extend to you and Mr. Burgess a popular reception in Faneuil Hall. You both deserved it, and it is gratifying to know that it met with your approbation. The fact that so many thousands of our people filled the hall and blocked the neighboring streets, anxious to take you and Mr. Burgess by the hand, shows how much you are appreciated.

With great respect,
Yours sincerely,
HUGH O'BRIEN.

www.ingramcontent.com/pod-product-compliance
Lightning Source LLC
Chambersburg PA
CBHW031442160426
43195CB00010BB/824